T0077484

CODED MESSAGES

CODED MESSAGES

How the CIA and NSA Hoodwink Congress and the People

Nelson McAvoy

Algora Publishing
New York

Library of Congress Cataloging-in-Publication Data —

McAvoy, Nelson, 1930-
    Coded messages: how the CIA and NSA hoodwink Congress and
the people / Nelson McAvoy.
        p. cm.
    Includes bibliographical references and index.
    ISBN 978-0-87586-814-1 (hard cover: alk. paper) — ISBN 978-
0-87586-813-4 (soft cover: alk. paper) — ISBN 978-0-87586-815-8
(ebook) 1. Intelligence service—United States—History. 2. United
States. Central Intelligence Agency—History. 3. United States.
National Security Agency—History. I. Title.
    JK468.I6M286 2010
    327.1273—dc22
                                    2010037689

Front cover: *Battle of Midway Memorial Picture*

Printed in the United States

This book is dedicated to Phillip R. Zimmermann, a true folk hero of the 20th century

Abbreviations, Special Terms, and Names

Abbreviations

AFS	Air Force Security Service, at Bolling Field after World War II
AFSA	Armed Forces Security Agency, predecessor to NSA during the Korean War
ARPA	Advanced Research Projects Agency
AWOL	Absent without leave
ASA	Army Security Agency
CIA	Central Intelligence Agency
COMINT	Communications Intelligence
DCI	Director of Central Intelligence. World War II coordinator of intelligence inside the White House
DoD	Department of Defense
DPRK	Democratic People's Republic of Korea (Communist North Korea)
Echelon	(Carnivore) NSA computer search engines for phone and email traffic analysis
FDR	Franklin Delano Roosevelt
FISA	Foreign Intelligence Surveillance Act
HUMINT	Human intelligence, getting information directly from (usually undercover) people
Hq.	Headquarters
IG	Inspector general
JN-25	Naval code used by Japan during World War II
KP	Kitchen police
KPA	Korean People's Army, Communist North Korea army prior the Korean conflict
DPRK	Democratic People's Republic of Korea, Communist North Korean State prior the Korean conflict
MAGIC	Japanese diplomatic code of World War II
MATS	Military air transport system
MOS	Military occupational specialty
MP	Military police
NCO	Non-commissioned officer
NKVD	The regular, public police force of the USSR 1934-1954, including traffic police, firefighting, border guards and archives
NSS	Naval Security Service, located in DC at Ward Circle on Nebraska Avenue
NSA	National Security Agency
OCS	Officer Candidate School

OD	Officer of the day
OSS	Office of Strategic Service. World War II operations behind enemy lines
PLA	People's Liberation Army, Chinese army that invaded Korea
PGP	Encryption software used throughout the world by the military and industrial and internet complex
PX	Post Exchange
RA	Regular army
RDF	Radio direction finding.
RTOP	research and technology operating plan
ROK	Republic of Korea
SAVAK	Iranian secret police under the Shah of Iran in the 1960s
SIS	Signals Intelligence Service, located at Arlington Hall Station during World War II
TDY	Temporary duty
TVA	Tennessee Valley Authority
USMT	U. S. Military Telegraph Corps
WAC	Women's Army Corps
WAVES	Women Accepted for Volunteer Emergency Service. Women naval personnel

Special Terms

Ammonia maser	A device which increases or produces electromagnetic waves, especially microwaves, where the medium is a beam of ammonium (NH_3)
Bug	A semi-automatic telegraph key
Fist	A telegraphy operator's unique transmission style

Names

Leonard Adleman	Co-inventor of the RSA public key algorithm
Dean G. Acheson	Secretary of State under President Truman
Robert O. Alde	Director of Research at NSA for 30 years
Dr. al-Balawi	Muslim extremist Jordanian who blew up himself and five CIA operatives in February 2010
Salvador Allende	Assassinated President of Chile
James Bamford	Author of three books on NSA

George A. Brownell, Esq.	Head of the committee to create NSA in 1951
Charles E. (Chip) Bohlen, Esq.	State Department, Assistant to George A. Brownell in forming NSA
William Crowell	Director of NSA
Whitfield Diffie	Co-inventor (with M.E. Hellman) of public key cryptography concept
Agnes Meyer Driscoll	World-renowned cryptanalysis
Lynn Falkner	High school teacher and naval officer during WW II
Eugene Fubini	1938 immigrant to the USA and Assistant Director of NSA
Martin Gardner	Science writer for *Scientific American*
General Michael Hayden	NSA Director from 1999 to 2005
Kelly Goen	Cryptographer who spread PGP as freeware
Boris Caesar Wilhelm Hagelin	Inventor of the crypto machine used by the US in World War II
Martin E. Hellman	Co-inventor (with Whitfield Diffie) of public key concept
William H. Jackson	Assistant to George A. Brownell in forming NSA
Harry Kidder	Prominent Naval NCO cryptanalysis during World War II
George Lakoff	UCLA Professor and renowned Cognitive Neuroscience authority
Steven Levy	Author of the book *Crypto*
Robert A. Lovett	Secretary of Defense under President Truman
General John Magruder	Assistant to George A. Brownell in forming NSA
Charlie Merritt	Renowned computer expert and cryptographer
Tom McCune	PGP expert
Ron Rivest	Co-inventor of the RSA public key algorithm
General Harry Reicheldorfer	ASA Commander, 1950
Joseph Rochefort	Director of the school for cryptanalyst during World War II
Adi Shamir	Co-inventor of the RSA public key cryptography algorithm
Anson Stager	Civil War USMT Director
Edwin Stanton	Secretary of War in 1861

General Walter Bedell Smith	Director of Central Intelligence during World War II
William Weisband	Soviet spy who infiltrated Arlington Hall Station during World War II
Phil Zimmermann	PGP inventor

TABLE OF CONTENTS

PREFACE

Since the formation of the National Security Agency in 1952, to my knowledge no employees or ex-employees have written books on their activities. In the last 60 years I have never heard an interviewer on radio or TV interview an NSA employee or retired NSA employee. Through all the intelligence successes and fiascos after World War II; through the Korean War; the Viet Nam War; the Bay of Pigs invasion of Cuba and the Cuban Missile Crisis; the invasion of Afghanistan after the 9/11 attack on the US; the unprovoked invasion, conquest, and occupation of Iraqi on the basis of false claims they had weapons of mass-destruction; I have never heard an interviewer on radio or TV, interview an NSA employee or retired NSA employee. No mention of the National Security Agency. The National Security Council, yes, but not NSA.

Through all the aforementioned intelligence successes and fiascoes, no Senate or Congressional Committee has ever subpoenaed an NSA employee or retired NSA employee. The Director of NSA volunteered to speak before certain Committees a few times but gave essentially no information regarding the activities of the Agency.

Then after the 2006 revelation by Mark Klein, a retired AT&T engineer, that AT&T had spliced off fiber optic cables in a Los Angeles telephone substation, it came out that NSA was keeping a copy of all email and phone calls. NSA was all over the news. Still, with all the national press, evening after evening, and all the print media coverage, there was never an interview of an NSA employee or retired NSA employee. Yet Congress passed a law as a result of these revelations to give AT&T and all other telecommunications companies immunity from prosecution.

In contrast, during these 60 years, Central Intelligence Agency Directors, employees, ex-employees, Division Chiefs and peripheral contractors by the thousands have been interviewed, subpoenaed, and have written books on CIA's detailed activities.

This contrast, the differences in the exposure of these two agencies and what the world knows about them, was planned into their creation. The clever way NSA and CIA have jointly arranged their exposure to the world will probably never be known if I do not tell the story. Part of the reason for this is that the story could not have been told prior to 1997; you'll see why as you read the book. And now, as far as I know, there is no one but me who is still around to tell the story. I would not like this part of history to be lost.

INTRODUCTION

It isn't necessary to be crazy to be a cryptanalysis, but it always helps.—Joseph Rochefort (from Op-20-G)

Once up on a time during the beginning years of the agricultural era in the fertile basin around the Mediterranean, there were two nomadic tribes. As usual, when they encountered each other, the elders shared a camp fire and exchanged gifts. One tribe mentioned that they had nine families each with six sheep. The other tribe had six families with nine sheep. It never occurred to the elders that both tribes had exactly the same number of sheep. Any fourth grader would know that. That $6 \times 9 = 9 \times 6$. You have never met a reasonably bright person who does not think this is trivial. It is not trivial, and millions of bright people to whom this was not obvious lived and died before algebra was commonplace. The multiplication tables and the basic ideas of algebra are not trivial or obvious unless you have been schooled in that perspective. If you think reciprocity of multiplication is a trivial concept, consider this: A monk leaves his habitat at sunrise and walks all day to his mountain retreat and arrives that evening. After a few days of prayer he leaves at sunrise and returns. Explain that it is trivial and obvious that the monk was at a place on the trail at exactly the same time of day on the trip up as he was on the trip back. For these and other concepts to become a trivial and obvious part of the culture takes a long time and an education process.

There are trivial and obvious aspects of our culture today that are unknown to the people and law makers of our country. There are some things in our culture that should be trivial and obvious to all, but are not. Most people would not see right off how trivial and obvious the solution to the monk problem is. As soon as you tell them to, in their mind's eye, let the monk go and come back on the same morning, i.e., move the return tip to the morning of the ascending trip, it becomes trivial and obvious that the two monks would have to pass each other on the trip up and the trip back. Now you easily see that the monk was at a place on the trail at exactly the same time on the trip up and the trip back. Now this will be just as trivial and obvious to you as 6x9 = 9x6.

Once I was involved in two separate sports activities; one was training horses and the other was training sheep dogs, border collies. When I was at a party with the horsy people and wanted to say something funny, I would say I was trying to teach my horse to catch a Frisbee. With the sheep dog people, I would say I was trying to teach my collie to trot and canter on command. We all know that species have natural inborn inclinations that lend themselves to certain types of training. One of the characteristics of human training, according to the findings in the new fields of Cognitive Science and Neuroscience, is that what we hear and see over and over again as we grow up becomes our common sense: no matter how unreasonable, bizarre, or violent it seems to the common sense of others.

Here are two areas of common sense shared by practically all Americans that have led us astray and that misguide our leaders. These are things that people have learned at their parents' knees that are no longer true plus misinformation from powerful institutions that have duped us all. Unlike foolish ideas that I and most others hold, and that are shared by part of the people, these two are almost universally believed by US citizens:

If the federal government, with their thousands of brilliant workers, billions of dollars to spend and the best and fastest computers in the world, wants to, it can decipher an encrypted email message from a child to you or an email message from one terrorist to another. They cannot. This is because of mathematical inventions in the 1979–89 era. The breaking of coded messages is as passé as a cavalry charge or a battleship in warfare.

People in the United States think that the Central Intelligence Agency (CIA) is one of the intelligence agencies of the US government and that the National Security Agency (NSA) has the main job of communications intelligence. Not so. CIA is our sabotage, clandestine war-waging, assassination, and provocateur agency. NSA is the US intelligence agency with a larger (classified) budget than CIA and the FBI put together.

This myth has been intentionally perpetrated by these agencies from their beginning. It was arranged in June 1952, when NSA was first formed. The unconstitutional lack of Congressional oversight granted to NSA when it was set up is no longer justified. One stunning example of the mindset of the 535 Senators and Congressmen and their staff is that they did not realize that the 9/11 Commission, set up jointly by the White House and Congress, did not interview or get information from any NSA personnel or even know that NSA was our primary intelligence organization. Yet practically all of the information gathered on those named as the perpetrators of 9/11 prior to their deed was obtained by NSA interceptors of plain text phone messages.[1] How did all of this come about?

> At 12:01 on the morning of November 4, 1952, a new federal agency was born. Unlike other such bureaucratic births, however, this one arrived in silence. No news coverage, no congressional debate, no press announcement, not even the whisper of a rumor Nor could any mention of the new organization be found in the Government Organization Manual or the Federal Register or the Congressional Record. Equally invisible were the new agency's director, its numerous buildings, and its ten thousand employees.
> Eleven days earlier, on October 24, President Harry S Truman scratched his signature on the bottom of a seven-page presidential memorandum addressed to Secretary of State Dean G. Acheson and Secretary of Defense Robert A. Lovett. . . , the order directed the establishment of an agency to be known as the National Security Agency. It was the birth certificate for America's newest and most secret agency, so secret in fact that only a handful in the government would be permitted to know of its existence."[2]

Sometime in the spring of 1953, word came down that the White House staff, under the new president, Dwight Eisenhower, had settled on the final arrangement such that:

NSA is the intelligence agency of the United States government. Neither Congress nor any other branch of the US

---

[1] *The Shadow Factory: The Ultra-Secret NSA from 9/11 to the Eavesdropping on America.* James Bamford. Doubleday, 2008, page 331.

[2] *The Puzzle Palace: Inside the National Security Agency, America's Most Secret Intelligence Organization.* James Bamford, Houghton Mifflin, 1983, page 1.

government is to be privy to the duties or budget of NSA, or have oversight thereof.

NSA is headed at least a lieutenant general or vice admiral, who answers to a Special Committee of the National Security Council consisting of the Secretary of Defense, the Secretary of State, and the President.

The specific duties of NSA were neither delineated by nor approved by Congress. NSA is subject to no congressional oversight, but their duties include all passive intelligence gathering, including infiltration.

Congress does have oversight over the CIA, and Congress was told that the CIA is the United States intelligence agency. But that was a lie. (This seemed a very reasonable thing to do at the time.)

The CIA was established to actually engage in all activities that result in changing situations directly, e.g., the arming of Afghanistan rebels as depicted in the movie "Charlie's War"; the secret US-led army in Laos during the Viet Nam war; mining the harbors of Nicaragua; the assassination of Chilean President Salvador Allende in 1973; the Bay of Pigs invasion; waterboarding and other torture of Iraqis, including their kidnapping and secret imprisonment and abuse in third countries; the buying and controlling foreign news media; et cetera.[5]

For over 60 years this ruse has worked beautifully: Intelligence was getting information. But Chilean President Salvador Allende was not assassinated to get information. The Bay of Pigs, Cuba, was not invaded in order to get information. The harbors of Nicaragua were not mined to get information. "Charlie's War" was not waged to get information. The secret army in Laos was not run to get information. The total 60 year history of the CIA has been that of a clandestine

---

[5] *The Invisible Government*, David Wise and Thomas B. Ross. Vintage Books, 1974.

provocateur with Congressional oversight. Yet news analyses always speak of them as our intelligence agency, as their name implies.

The CIA was formed two years before the NSA to replace the Office of Strategic Service of World War II fame. The NSA was to include the signal intelligence duties of the three services, the Army Security Agency, located at Arlington Hall Station (of World War II code-breaking fame); the Naval Security Service, located in DC at Ward Circle on Nebraska Avenue, and the Air Force Security Service at Bolling Field. A meeting was held at Arlington Hall Station, chaired by General Harry Reicheldorfer, Army Security Agency (ASA) Commander. The above information describing the functions of the CIA and the NSA was discussed in detail. The novelty of these ideas was discussed in the offices of Arlington Hall Station for months thereafter. How do I know this? I am one of the few persons at that first meeting who is still here today.

It soon became apparent that this was a very reasonable and wise arrangement. It was openly recognized that withdrawing Congress's right of oversight was unconstitutional. It was strongly held, though, that the end justified the means because the recent history of World War II had shown that years and millions of lives had been saved by code breaking which, of course, only worked if secrecy was guaranteed. It was imperative that there not be even a hint that an adversary's messages were being decrypted. NSA employees were not allowed to tell outsiders that they worked for NSA or "No Such Agency," as we used to say. No contract personnel were used and all NSA employees were either career civil servants or career military personnel.

There has to be some kind of cover system for the dissemination of NSA's end product, information, that would be used by other parts of the Government; and the CIA was a natural for the "cut out."

The NSA has a cadre of people versed in all main languages and dialects in the world. Not only that, they are versed in the customs, slang, dress, and politics of each country. They are comprised of military and civilians from age 20 to 70 of both genders and international heritage. Where else in the US Government would you have such a pool of talent for surreptitious snooping in other countries? There is a saying in COMINT (communications intelligence): sometimes the cheapest way to break a strong cipher is by greasing (the palm, by infiltration). In general, NSA people are just not the kind of people who would want to be associated with programs of assassination, torture and such aggressive behavior. The aggressive and passive functions would not mix under the same recruitment and administrative organization. And there would be no way to keep the "left hand" from knowing what the "right hand" does. So separation on the basis of aggressive and non-aggressive was a very natural and prudent thing to do.

But now there is no such activity of deciphering encrypted messages by the government or anyone else. Just as the invention of airplanes made the use of battleships obsolete, the invention of the RSA public key encryption algorithms in 1977, by three MIT professors, Ron Rivest, Adi Shemir, and Leonard Adleman; has eliminated the possibility of deciphering the origin or context of email messages today. NSA's reasons for not having congressional oversight have vanished. By downloading software from www.pgp.com (or preferable from http://www.philzimmermann.com/EN/sales/index.html); and by signing up for re-mailing your email at www.ultimate-anonymity.com or a similar place; any two world citizens with laptop computers can email each other completely privately and securely with no possibility of NSA or anybody else being able to discern the sender, content, or receiver (at least for 5000 years). Furthermore, when the laptops are turned off, there is no way confiscators can find out the content of the laptops if the owner has Universal PGP software in it. This fact negates the justification for NSA to be exempt from congressional oversight. To quote from Tom McCune's web page:

> It is important for all Internet users to understand that regular email offers no privacy, and can actually be read by many people other than who it is sent to. Your Internet service provider (ISP) probably keeps a copy on its computers, copies of emails sent from a network computer (such as at work or school) are probably kept behind, and all of the Internet computers the email goes through on its way to the recipient can keep a copy. The administrators of all these computers can read your email if they choose to, and they can send it to anyone they might want to. The US government and other governments routinely intercepts email and scans it for interesting words or phrases (Echelon—Carnivore). With PGP encryption, all of these people can have free access to our email, and still have no idea as to its content—this is real privacy.[4]

As to the protection from NSA, William Crowell, Deputy Director of NSA said on March 20, 1997:

> "If all the personal computers in the world—260 million—were put to work on a single PGP-encrypted message, it would still take an estimated 12 million times the age of the universe, on average, to break a single message."

---

[4] http://www.mccone.cc/PGP2.htm#Why

Pathetically, Congress is still being hoodwinked by NSA and the Executive branch of the US government. The main reason that Congress is still hoodwinked by the Executive is not because information is not available; information is available. It is because of the way our minds work, or really, don't work. This has become apparent from the consequence of findings in Cognitive Science studies.[5] Living systems must categorize. Since we are neural beings, our categories are formed through our embodiment (Author's note: another term for embodiment is brain circuits). What that means is that the categories we form are part of our experiences! They are the structures that differentiate aspects of our experience into discernible kinds. Categorization is thus not a purely intellectual matter, occurring after the fact of experience. Rather, the formation and use of categories is the stuff of experience. It is part of what our bodies and brains are constantly engaged in. We cannot, as some meditative traditions suggest, 'get beyond' our categories and have a purely uncategorized and unconceptualized experience. Neural beings cannot do that.

We, and our parents, grew up with exciting stories lived by our grandparents and their parents. The breathtaking stories of wars and spies and battles that hinged on the making and breaking of ciphers. The author has heard some of these legends of the all-powerful government code breaking apparatus. But he worked at the heart of that apparatus and did not find it all-powerful at all. In this book I hope to share with you some of the categories that are the stuff of my experiences. This book provides a detailed explanation of these ideas and will walk you through the concepts of traditional cryptography, and thence to public key cryptography. Then

---

[5] *Philosophy in the Flesh: The Embodied Mind and Its Challenge to Western Thought*, George Lakoff. Basic Books, 1999, page 19.

we explain how cryptography moved from the government-only purview to predominately a commercial endeavor.

This is a gripping story of how NSA tried to squelch public key cryptography. Thanks to Phil Zimmermann, a folk hero of the modern era, they could not. Had they been successful, there would be no Internet as we know it. No e-commerce. Trust is the essence of commerce and trust is brought to the Internet by public key crypto. I sent my credit card number to Saudi Arabia, automatically encrypted in public key cryptography, with complete confidence to buy a $5 head scarf. With this background we hope to modify your "neural categories" to more clearly see the way things really are in the area of message privacy.

I am not implying that the NSA has ever done anything that is not honorable and proper. I am proud of my time spent at the agency and my work there was always with beloved compadres. But now it is time for Congressional oversight.

The days are gone when withholding Congressional oversight could be found reasonable and justifiable. In 1997, the NSA went from all civil service and career military employees to 70% contract employees because there ceased to be a need for the obsession with ultra secrecy. There is a far greater need to protect the constitutional rights of citizen privacy today than in the past. Today, everyone in the world can have a "thumb" drive to plug into any computer with a USB port and have a dossier of everyone in the United States. They hold 128 Gigabits of information and cost little to nothing.

Protecting personal privacy is part of the business of Congress and the Fourth Amendment of the Constitution of the United States, to wit: "The right of the people to be secure in their persons, houses, papers, and effects, against unreasonable searches and seizures, shall not be violated, and no Warrants shall issue, but upon probable cause, supported by

Oath or affirmation, and particularly describing the place to be searched, and the persons or things to be seized."

Congress can no longer play dumb. They must change the law so they have the right and obligation to know what the NSA does.

United States Civil War

A symmetric code is one where the sender and receiver have the same code book for encryption and decryption. It is what one typically thinks of as crypto. During the Civil War the newly formed Signal Corps under Brigadier General Albert Myer was in charge of communications for the Union Army. Secretary of War, Edwin Stanton dismissed General Myer as Chief Signal Officer Nov. 10, 1863, and reassigned him to duty in Memphis, Tenn. The problem was that General Myer did not understand cryptography and the importance of ciphers and codebook security and secrecy. Encryption was too serious to be left to the Army. In reassigning Gen. Myer, Stanton also turned over all telegraphic responsibilities to a civilian operated U.S. Military Telegraph Corps (USMT). USMT employed civilian telegraphy operators and was managed by a civilian, Anson Stager, directly under Secretary of War Edwin Stanton.

Anson Stager, a 21-year-old, was hired to telegraph in 1846. A line was constructed between Harrisburg, Pa., and Philadelphia, Pa., which Stager was placed in charge of the Lancaster, Pa., station. As telegraphy lines expanded, so did Stager's responsibilities. Stager moved to Ohio to manage telegraph lines there and eventually served as the first general superintendent of Western Union Telegraph Company, newly formed in 1856. During the period leading up to the Civil War, a host of telegraph and railroad agencies employed ciphers in their telegraphic messages.

General Sherman	Black
Division	Wharton
Tennessee River	Godwin
Midnight	Mary
Advance	Wafer
Attack	Walden
General Bragg	Quadrant
Fortifications	Saginaw
Capture	Wayland
Chattanooga	Jasmine
Wounded	Whist
Killed	Walrus
Arms	Randolph
Artillery	Richard
Ammunition	Ramsay
General Grant	Bangor
6 p.m.	Jennie

Figure 1.1. Elements of the code book used by General Grant's cipher clerk for messages to Headquarters in Washington DC.

More often than not, the telegraph operators themselves devised these early ciphers and so they were this nation's cryptographic pioneers. Stager developed a very simple cipher system, yet it was never broken by the Confederacy. In fact, the Confederacy was so baffled by Stager's ciphers that intercepted messages were often placed in Southern newspapers in hopes that someone could decipher them. For example, using a Stager cipher, here's a possible message that Gen. Ulysses Grant could have sent to Gen. William Sherman in November 1863 during the battle of Chattanooga:

> To General Sherman,
>
> Your division will cross the Tennessee River at midnight and advance and attack General Bragg's fortifications, then capture Chattanooga. Please advise on wounded, killed, arms, artillery, rations and ammunition.
>
> General Grant, 6 p.m.

The telegraph operator would look in the USMT codebook and put the appropriate "arbitraries" into this message. The arbitraries from the codebook are listed in Figure 1.1.

The message with the corresponding arbitraries would be:

> To BLACK your WHARTON will cross GODWIN at MARY and WAFER and WALDEN QUADRANT SAGINAW then WAYLAND JASMINE. Please advise on WHIST, WALRUS, RANDOLPH, RICHARD, rations and RAMSAY. BANGOR. JENNIE.

The message then was broken down into a division of five lines and six columns, Figure 1.2. Thus, Grant's message would be enciphered going up the sixth column, down the fifth, up the fourth, down the third, up the second and down the first. This zigzag route was code named "Congress." The telegraph operator would append CONGRESS as the first word in the message. The resulting message would then be sent over the telegraph as:

CONGRESS JENNIE RANDOLPH JASMINE AND CROSS WILL WAFER WAYLAND WALRUS BANGOR RAMSAY WHIST THEN AND WHAR-TON YOUR MARY SAGINAW ON AND RATIONS ADVISE QUADRANT AT BLACK TO GODWIN WALDEN PLEASE RICHARD.

To	Black	Your	Wharton	Will	Cross
Godwin	At	Mary	And	Wafer	And
Walden	Quadrant	Saginaw	Then	Wayland	Jasmine
Please	Advise	On	Whist	Walrus	Randolph
Richard	Rations	And	Ramsay	Bangor	Jennie

Figure 1.2. The message written out before commutation.

Col. Anson Stagers had designated that only 14 individuals have access to this cipher, including only one cipher clerk under Gen. Grant's command and a cipher clerk at the War Department Headquarters. Access was not available to President Lincoln, not General Grant or any of their staff. General Grant learned this the hard way to the chagrin of one of his cipher clerks, Corporal Samuel H. Beckwith. As General Grant tells it in his memoirs:

I was obliged to leave the telegraphic operator back at Nashville, because that was the point at which all dispatches to me would come, to be forwarded from there. As I have said, it was necessary for me also to have an operator during this inspection who had possession of this cipher to enable me to telegraph to my division and to the War Department without my dispatches being read by all the operators along the line of wires over which they were transmitted. Accordingly I ordered the cipher operator to turn over the key to Captain Cyrus B. Comstock, of the Corps of Engineers, whom I had selected as a wise and discreet man who certainly could be trusted with the cipher if the operator at my headquarters could. The operator (Beckwith) refused point blank to turn over the key to Captain Comstock as directed by me, stating that his orders from the War Department were not to give it to anybody—the commanding general or any one else. I told him I would see whether he would or not. He said that if he did he would be punished. I told him if he did not he most certainly would be punished. Finally, seeing that punishment was certain if he refused longer to obey my order, and being somewhat remote (even if he was not protected altogether from the consequences of his disobedience to his orders) from the War Department, he yielded. When I returned from Knoxville I found quite a commotion. The operator had been reprimanded very severely and ordered to be relieved. I informed the Secretary of War, or his assistant secretary in charge of the telegraph, Stager, that the man could not be relieved, for he had only obeyed my orders. It was absolutely necessary for me to have the cipher, and the man would most certainly have been punished if he had not delivered it; that they would have to punish me if they punished anybody, or words to that effect.[6]

What really happened was as follows:

From his headquarters in Nashville, Tennessee, Grant notified General-in-Chief H.W. Halleck (the rough equivalent of today's Chief of Staff of the Army) in Washington by telegram on 20 January 1864:

---

[6] *Personal Memoirs*, Ulysses S. Grant, Chapter XLV. Kessinger Publishing, LLC, 2005.

I have ordered the cipher operator to give the Washington cipher to Colonel Comstock [of Grant's staff]. The necessity of this I felt whilst in East Tennessee, receiving dispatches I could not read until I returned. The operator received the following dispatch from Colonel Stager to Colonel [Samuel] Bruch [departmental head of the USMT]: 'Beckwith [Grant's telegrapher-code clerk] must not instruct any one in the cipher. An order will be issued and sent to you on this subject. I protest against Colonel Stager's interference. I shall be as cautious as I possibly can, that improper persons do not get the key to official correspondence.

Halleck responded to Grant by telegram the same afternoon:

The Secretary of War directs that you report by telegraph the facts and circumstances of the act of Lieutenant-Colonel Comstock, in requiring A.C. [sic: Samuel H.] Beckwith, telegraphic cipher clerk, to impart to

Figure 1.3. Typical Civil War communications wagon. It would be connected to a telegraph line at an army headquarters.

him (Colonel Comstock) the secret cipher, entrusted to said Beckwith for use exclusively in your correspondence with the War Department and Headquarters of the Army.

Grant replied the next day:

I ordered Beckwith to give Colonel Comstock the key to Washington cipher, in order that I might have always some one with me who had it. Whilst at Knoxville I experienced the disadvantage of not having given such an order before. I would recommend that a cipher be used not known to Colonel Stager or any operator.

Colonel Stager's apologetic explanation to General Halleck is also dated 21 January:

The information furnished me led me to believe that the request of the staff officer for a copy of the cipher was without General Grant's authority, and as a new cipher had been arranged expressly for Mr. Beckwith's use at General Grant's headquarters, with the order of the Secretary of War recently issued that the operators for this duty should be held responsible for strict privacy in its use, I initiated the message referred to, not thinking that it would come in conflict with General Grant's orders or wishes, the general having recently expressed his entire satisfaction with Mr. Beckwith's services. I am exceedingly mortified at the result, as my only desire was to furnish the most reliable means of communication to General Grant with the War Department. The new cipher was arranged with a view of being used by telegraph experts, and it is believed cannot be used with any success by others than telegraphers. A great number of errors have been made by staff officers working ciphers, owing to their lack of experience in telegraphic characters, and it is believed that greater accuracy can be secured by placing ciphers in the hands of experts selected for this duty. The new cipher differs in many respects from those formerly used, and the one arranged for General Grant should not be known to any other party, hence my anxiety to keep it in Beckwith's hands. I sincerely regret that General Grant is led to believe that it is willful interference on my part.

Halleck informed Grant on 22 January 1864:

It was known that the contents of telegrams communicated by means of existing ciphers have been made public without authority. As these ciphers have been communicated to a number of persons the Department was unable to discover the delinquent individual. To obviate this difficulty a new and very complicated cipher was prepared for communications between you and the War Department, which, by direction of the Secretary of War, was to be communicated to only two individuals, one at your headquarters and one in the War Department. It was to be confided to no one else, not even to me or any member of my staff." Mr. Beckwith, who was sent to your headquarters, was directed by the Secretary of War to communicate this cipher to no one. In obeying Colonel Comstock's orders he disobeyed the Secretary and has been dismissed. He should have gone to prison if Colonel Comstock had seen fit to put him there. Instead of forcing the cipher from him in violation of the orders of the War Department, Colonel Comstock should have reported the facts of the case here for the information of the Secretary of War, who takes the personal supervision and direction of the military telegraphs. On account of this cipher having been communicated to Colonel Comstock the Secretary has directed another to be prepared in its place, which is to be communicated to no one, no matter what his rank, without his special authority.

The Secretary does not perceive the necessity of communicating a special cipher, intended only for telegrams to the War Department, to members of your staff any more than to my staff or to the staff officers of other generals commanding geographical departments. All your communications with others are conducted through the ordinary cipher. It was intended that Mr. Beckwith should accompany you wherever you required him, transportation being furnished for that purpose. If by any casualty be separated from you, communication could be kept up by the ordinary cipher till the vacancy could be supplied.

It is to be regretted that Colonel Comstock interfered with the orders of the War Department in this case. As stated in former instructions, if any telegraphic employee should not give satisfaction he should be reported, and, if there be a pressing necessity, he may be suspended. But as the corps of telegraphic operators receive their instructions directly from the Secretary of War, these instructions should not be interfered with except under very extraordinary circumstances, which should be immediately reported.

P.S. Colonel Stager is the confidential agent of the Secretary of War, and directs all telegraphic matters under his orders.

Grant responded to Halleck on 4 February:

Your letter of the 22nd, inclosing copy of Colonel Stager's of the 21st to you, is received. I have also circular or order, dated January 1, 1864, postmarked Washington, January 23, and received on the 29th.

I will state that Beckwith is one of the best of men. He is competent and industrious. In the matter for which he has been discharged, he only obeyed my orders and could not have done otherwise than he did and remain. Beckwith has always been employed at headquarters as an operator, and I have never thought of taking him with me except when headquarters are moved. On the occasion of my going to Knoxville, I received Washington dispatches which I could not read until my return to this place. To remedy this for the future I directed Colonel Comstock to acquaint himself with the cipher.

Beckwith desired to telegraph Colonel Stager on the subject before complying with my direction. Not knowing of any order defining who and who alone could be entrusted with the Washington cipher, I then ordered Beckwith to give it to Colonel Comstock and to inform Colonel Stager of the fact that he had done so. I had no thought in this matter of violating any order or even wish of the Secretary of War. I could see no reason why I was not as capable of selecting the proper person to entrust with this secret as Colonel Stager. In fact, I thought nothing further of this, other than that Colonel Stager had his operators under such discipline that they were afraid to obey orders from any one but himself without knowing first his pleasure.

Beckwith has been dismissed for obeying my order. His position is important to him and a better man cannot be selected for it. I respectfully ask that Beckwith be restored.

When Colonel Stager's directions were received here the cipher had already been communicated. His order was signed by himself and not by the Secretary of War. It is not necessary for me to state that I am a stickler for form, but will obey any order or wish of my superior, no matter how conveyed, if I know, or only think it came from him. In this instance I supposed Colonel Stager was acting for himself and without the knowledge of any one else.

Having satisfied Washington, Grant received on 10 February a telegram from Halleck that stated, among other things unrelated, "Mr. Beckwith has been restored."

A similar incident happened to me at Arlington Hall Station, the center for code breaking for the US Army in World War II. The Officer of the Day (OD) was in charge evenings and weekends. All field grade officers were rotated into this duty about once a month. The Non Commissioned Officer (NCO) to the OD each night took a locked briefcase to the code room of the Pentagon, just three miles away. From Arlington Hall one goes down Glebe Road to Shirley Highway, thence to the Pentagon. As Duty NCO one evening, I was tooling along at what I thought was the speed limit. An Arlington County motorcycle policeman pulled me over and said, "You're speeding, Sergeant, let me see your driver's license." I handed him the Department of Defense (DoD) driver's license and he said, "That's not a proper driver's license. You're in a civilian car. I'll have to take you in." I put the Colt .45 (issued for the night) into view and explained as non-threateningly as possible that I had orders to shoot anyone who separated me from the briefcase. I did not think about whether to shoot him, even though I had visions running through my head of two little tykes playing in the yard of the policeman's bungalow and a fun wife watching over them. I knew I had to do it. My thoughts were how I could make it the least painful for him. A Colt .45 is a very formidable weapon. Fortunately for him and a very shook-up sergeant, he said, "Watch your speeding," and drove off.

The history of crypto has been centered round the protection of code books and machines used for encryption and decryption keys. Only symmetric codes were used prior to 1977. The code book, the protocol, the cipher machines, the algorithms, are identical and hopefully, only in the possessions of both the senders and receivers. In contradistinction, an antisymmetric system, also known as public key crypto, which is used exclusively today, has no code book and there is no intrigue or precarious or surreptitious aspect. Everyone who uses crypto has a number that is published just as a phone number in a phone book is. This public number is used to encrypt the key for the message sent. No more code books, no more intrigue, game over.

Associated with the public number (actually two numbers) is a private number generated by the receiver and kept secret by her. This number is never passed, or even written down, or given to anyone. The private key is in the receiver's computer and can be pulled up by a pass-phrase known only to the receiver. It is the responsibility of each person to take care of her own pass phrase for her private key. The pass phrase is more than just a pass-word used commonly in computers. It is a long phrase chosen from the receiving person's long-term memory. In addition, everyone used the same procedure to encrypt and decrypt messages, be they national governments or eBay purchasers, friend and foe alike. This is an important distinction and a difficult adjustment for lay people to make. Before going into an explanation of public key crypto, we give another example of a classic symmetric cipher. We use this example because it gets us closer to modern ciphers that have plain text represented by blocks of numbers that are modularly added to random number blocks.

The Battle of Midway: World War II Symmetric Code JN-25

The JN-25 was the name the US Navy cryptographers gave to the Japanese Navy crypto system used from 1935 on through World War II. We tell the story of JN-25 for many reasons:

- It is a gut-wrenching story of how a few exciting people changed the world and became book-worm heroes.

- It showed for the first time how a crypto system completely changed the course of a war.

- It was a numerical system like today's systems and it gives us a crypto reference to explain our present day anti-symmetric, i.e. public key systems.

- It shows how traffic analysis goes along with crypt-analysis and how the present day equivalent of direction-finding (DF) plays a roll.

I can tell the story in ways that no one else can because I knew many of the cast of characters and the feelings of the people of the time. I worked at Arlington Hall Station and enticed many to talk about "the olden days" although it was not kosher for them to do so.

In the spring of 1920, FBI agents noticed that the assistant council of the Japanese Consulate in New York City periodically would catch the train to all coastal cities on the west coast as well as the east. They notified the Office of Naval Intelligence (ONI). Radio messages sent from the Consulate were encrypted. From late 19th century to 1940, the police department of east coast cities and the officer corps of the US Army and Navy were more than half micks (of Irish and Scottish ancestry). The Italian and East European immigrants were just as prevalent in the population, but to get jobs with the authorities, one had to read and write English. So a particularly cozy relation existed between New York City Police (NYCP) and many in the ONI. The NYCP, as was common, had a benevolence fund. It was a charity fund for the families of fallen officers and such. Money came in by hook or crook, fund raisers, and quasi-charitable contributions from local businesses. What ONI wanted them to do was a god-send for the shenanigan, I mean benevolence, fund. ONI had a slush fund in the Riggs Bank in Washington, DC. The NYCP took the job of getting the Consulate's code book with gusto. They would have a street dance in front of the Consulate while electricians and janitors plied their trade of picking locks and photographing pages of the code book. The book had about 100,000 entries, like a dictionary, with a four-digit number alongside each. This was the "Imperial Japanese Navy Secret Operating Code–1918."

But all was not well because the code book was of little value without the additive book that was not kept in the safe at the Consulate. The crypto system used by the Japanese Navy throughout World War I and World War II was the same. You could think of the code book as a dictionary with a 4-digit number attached to each entry. Before transmissions, these 4-digit number groups were first written out into a message. There was a second book, an additive book. The additive book was nothing more than a book of four-digit random numbers. Any (meaningful) number, added to a random number will give you a random number. We will use 5-digit numerals for our example because they upgraded to JN-25. Let's take for example 37251, the number for "admiral" in the message below. Now let's go to the additive book and get a five-digit random number. For our example we go to www.random.org on the net and get a few and pretend they are our additive book:

18061	31229	24665	32324	72336
42769	89356	29095	47576	18139
65306	48503	73936	69115	38315
64696	53276	74471	63248	16935
93997	25001	13224	45122	34578
63979	90608	33643	83849	77939
26268	16906	96811	16374	56759
73115	54010	15991	29359	76572
69148	63030	13594	41988	69102

Figure 1.7. Our sample for additive book associated with the code book.

We add the random number to the number in the message. But we do not carry the 1 as in arithmetic. They called this "false adding and subtracting". It is really modular arithmetic as described in Appendix A and is used in crypto ad nauseam. In other words, 5+6=1(mod 10) and 8-9=9(mod 10). Think of (mod 10) arithmetic as moving the hand on a clock with 10 hours as shown below. On the clock, 2+11=3. 2-3=9, 2-5=7, 6+6=2, 6+35= 1.

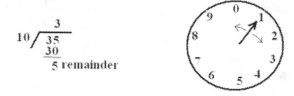

Suppose the message is that Admiral Takora requests detailed list. This would be:

Admiral	Takora	requests	detailed	list	message
37251	21768	83674	56214	48615	message from code book
65306	48503	73936	69115	38315	random number
92557	69261	56500	15329	76920	add random number for encrypted message
37251	21768	83674	56214	48515	subtract random number for decrypting

Also, each message contained a key that told the receiver where to begin in the additive book to decode the message. In our example it was line 3. This might not seem like a substantial crypto system. Indeed it is excellent, almost impenetrable. It is completely impenetrable if the random numbers of the additive book are used once and never used again. It is completely unbreakable because a number added (false adding) to a random number is a random number. For example, we can take the three columns of five digit random numbers, below and use false addition as follows:

19807	36236	93423	39207	21154
60393	30244	65200	56741	56422
10725	27967	69252	33072	16297

Adding the first row of random numbers to 12345:
21142=12345+19807
48571=12345+36236
05768=12345+93423
41542=12345+39207
33499=12345+21154.

Adding the second row of random numbers to 12345:
72638=12345+60393
42589=12345+30244
77545=12345+65200
68086=12345+56741
68767=12345+56422.

Adding the third row of random numbers to 12345.
22060=12345+10725
39202=12345+27967
71597=12345+69252
45317=12345+33072
28532=12345+16297.

You can see that in these 15 numbers, there is no 12345 pattern to the sum. You can also see that if the random numbers are subtracted (falsely) from the sum, one always gets 12345.

In addition to the problem of not having the additive book, there was a bigger problem of having no Japanese linguist or radiomen who could receive "Japanese".

The Japanese katakana syllabary was derived from abbreviated Chinese characters used by Buddhist monks to indicate the correct pronunciations of Chinese texts in the 9th century. At first there were many different symbols to represent one syllable of spoken Japanese, but over the years the system was streamlined. By the 14th century, there was a more or less one-to-one correspondence between spoken and written syllables.

The word katakana means "part (of kanji) syllabic script." The "part" refers to the fact that katakana characters represent parts of kanji. The katakana syllabary consists of 48 syllables and it was originally considered "men's writing." In each column below, the romaji or sound appears on the left, the katakana symbols in the middle and the old Chinese kanji from which the symbols (technically syllabary) were derived on the right. We include the kanji only for completeness.

カタカナ = katakana

a	ア	阿	i	イ	伊	u	ウ	宇	e	エ	江	o	オ	於
ka	カ	加	ki	キ	幾	ku	ク	久	ke	ケ	介	ko	コ	己
sa	サ	散	shi	シ	之	su	ス	須	se	セ	世	so	ソ	曽
ta	タ	多	chi	チ	千	tsu	ツ	川	te	テ	天	to	ト	止
na	ナ	奈	ni	ニ	二	nu	ヌ	奴	ne	ネ	祢	no	ノ	乃
ha	ハ	八	hi	ヒ	比	fu	フ	不	he	ヘ	部	ho	ホ	保
ma	マ	万	mi	ミ	三	mu	ム	牟	me	メ	女	mo	モ	毛
ya	ヤ	也				yu	ユ	由				yo	ヨ	輿
ra	ラ	良	ri	リ	利	ru	ル	流	re	レ	礼	ro	ロ	呂
wa	ワ	和	wi	ヰ	井				we	ヱ	恵	wo	ヲ	乎
												n	ン	无

Figure 1.4. On the left is the Roman alphabet sound, in the middle is the Japanese katakana syllable (syllabary), and on the right is the ancient Kanji Chinese syllabary.

Just as the Latin alphabet has the Morse Code for radio messages, e.g., a ●—, b —●●● , c —●—● , d —●● , e ● , f ●●—● , g —●● , h ●●●● , i ●● , j ●——— , k —●— , l ●—●● , m —— , n —● , o ——— , p ●——● , q ——●— , r ●—● , s ●●● , t— , u ●●— , v ●●●— , w ●—— カタカナ —, y —●— —, z ——●● , the Japanese have a カタカナ code.

MORSE	LETTER	カタカナ
. —	A	I
. —.—	AA	RO
. —.—.	AR	N
. —...	AS	O
. —.——	AW	TE
. —.———..	AWI	DE
—...	B	HA
—.....	BI	BA
—.....——.	BUN	PA
—.—.	C	NI
—..	D	HO
—.....	DI	BO
—.....——.	DUN	PO
.	E	HE
...	EI	BE
...——.	EUN	PE
..—..	ID	TO
.—.	F	CHI
——.	G	RI
....	H	NU
..	I	I

.———	J	WO
—.—	K	KA
——	M	YO
——..—	MW	A
—.	N	TA
—.———	NO	E
————	O	RE
————.—	OA	SU
.——.	P	TSU
——.—	Q	NE
.—.	R	NA
...	S	RA
—	T	MU
—.—..	TL	KI
..—	U	U
...—	V	KU
.——	W	YA
—..—	X	MA
—.—.	XE	MO
—.—	Y	KE
——..	Z	FU
——....	ZI	BU
——...——.	ZUN	PU
—..——	ZT	HI
—..———..	ZTI	BI
—..—..——.	ZTUN	PI

Figure 1.5. The Japanese katakana (syllables) syllabary as used in Morse Code telegraphy. The "syllabary" works like our alphabet and syllables are used the way we use letters.

This is how they sent keyed messages in the plain text. For example, if they wanted to send the word katakana, they would send ▬ ▪ ▬　▬ ▪　▬ ▪ ▬　▪ ▬ ▪, usually with a very crisp, beautiful fist. (The word "fist" is to telegraphy as "voice" is to speech.)

In other words, the Japanese telegraphers used a different "Morse code" than we did.

Today it might seem surprising that ONI had no Japanese linguist that they could trust, but at the time it was not. They hired Dr. Emerson J. Haworth and his wife, who both taught Japanese at local colleges, to translate the katakana into English. The military genera presented a problem, but by 1924 they had produced a dictionary, grammar book and a code book in English, arranged in both alphabetical order and code number order. The books were beautifully bound in red buckram cloth; hence the name history has given them, The Red Book.

The Red Book was handed over to the Office of Naval Communications. Surprisingly, the US Navy had no organized code breaking program. So in January 1924 they set up Op-20-G for code breaking and creation of our Navy's ciphers. It consisted of two people, Lieutenant Laurence F. Safford and Agnes Driscoll. By war's end there would be 5,000 workers there. The two of them had become the creators of naval cryptography.

Staffo, as he was affectionately and respectfully called, had ranked 14th in the Naval Academy's class of 1916. His language skills had landed him in command of a Yangtze River mine sweeper. That and his mathematical skills had landed him the Op-20-G at the outset. Op was operations, Op-20 was communications and G was just the 7th Section in the Navy's communications office. Some of Staffo's mates used to laugh and said he never looked neat and tidy. No one was more neat and tidy of mind and organization, for sure.

Figure 1.6. Battle of Midway Memorial Picture

> The WACs and WAVEs will win the war, parlez vous,
> The WACs and WAVEs will win the war, parlez vous,
> The WACs and WAVEs will win the war,
> So what the heck are we fighting for?
> Inkie dinky stinky parlez vous.

Well, at least one WAVE I know helped win the war, and that was Agnes Driscoll.

Agnes Driscoll (née Meyer) was born in 1889 and in 1911 she graduated from Ohio State University; majoring in mathematics, physics, foreign languages, and music. From her earliest days as a college student, Agnes Meyer pursued technical and scientific studies atypical for a woman of the times.

This made her somewhat of a loner, although she was very gregarious and talkative. After graduation, she moved to Texas where she was music director of the Amarillo Military Academy.

In June 1918, Agnes Meyer enlisted in the United States Navy. She was recruited at the highest possible rank of chief yeoman(F) and was assigned to the Code and Signal section of the Director of Naval Communications. In 1918, women all went into the Navy as Yeoman(F). She served a four-year hitch as a "yeomanette." As a code clerk in the Navy Department in 1921, she encountered the first mechanical encryption rotor machine. It was invented and patented by Edward Hebern, who had opened a company in California and was trying to sell the machine to the Navy. He had told the Navy that it was unbreakable. Miss Meyer broke it in minimal time. Hebern hired her when she mustered out of the Navy. They did not get along too well; she soon quit, and married Michael B. Driscoll, a Washington attorney. Admiral Layton in his memoirs said of her,

> During my stint as head of the translation section of Op-20-G that I came to appreciate the magnitude of the contribution being make to our code-breaking by Mrs. Driscoll. I had been warned not to patronize Madam "X" as her colleges sometimes referred to her because she was sensitive to her role as a woman in a man's world. Because of this she kept to herself as much as possible and none of us were ever invited to socialize with her and her lawyer husband. While she could be warm and friendly, she usually affected an air of intense detachment which was heightened by her tailored clothes and shunning of makeup. It was surprising to hear Miss Aggie curse, which she frequent did—as fluently as any sailor whom I have ever heard. ...In the navy she was without peer as a cryptanalyst. [7]

[7] *And I Was There*, Edwin T. Layton, Quill Publishing, 1987, page 58.

That seems a bit unfair to me. I feel a little undercurrent of sexism here. With me she was warm and friendly and she laughed at my corny jokes. When I mentioned her name to old "On The Roof Gang" (I'll tell you later who they were) operators, they would just laugh and say, "*** a mighty." She tried to curse like a sailor but never could. They just loved her and they certainly did not call her Madam X behind her back as the officers did. There was no question as to her genius. Admiral Layton also said: "The patrician 'Miss Aggie,' as friends still called her, was tall, slender, quiet, and extremely dedicated. She not only trained most of the leading naval cryptanalysts of World War II, but they were all agreed that none exceeded her gifted accomplishments in the business."

Op-20-G had eight immediate tasks:

- Devise ciphers for the US Navy to use.

- Train radiomen in the reception of the katakana syllabary. (Navy slang henceforth will just be "kana.")

- Teach cryptanalysis.

- Recruit sailors and officers for this very highly specialized work.

- Arrange for training in Japanese language of Officers and men with secret clearance.

- Set up listening sites for traffic interception and direction-finding.

- Arrange for transfer of received messages to be available for analysis.

- Set up crypto analysis and end-product dissemination units.

The Navy was quite fortunate that the original Op-20-G compliment complimented each other so well. Lieutenant Safford was very non-threatening to people and could get them enthusiastically behind his tasks. Also, his contacts as a

World War I naval officer were priceless. So items 4 through 8 above were his bailiwick. He saw to it that promising officers were sent to the language school in Tokyo and that their next assignment was with Op-20-G (after sea duty, every other assignment for naval officers had to be sea duty). He set up competitions for breaking codes and similar feats in the literature read by navy personnel. Those that showed promise were assigned to Op-20-G. The first three items were handed over to Miss Aggie.

It was not until 1924 that the U.S. Navy had any operators that could receive Katakana. Then Chief Radioman Harry Kidder, stationed in the Philippines took it upon himself to learn. With the help of a shipmate's Japanese wife, he learned the katakana syllabary, taught himself the telegraphic equivalents of all the katakana characters, and began to intercept Japanese messages. He ended up in 1928 as director for training operators to receive Japanese traffic at Op-20-G. The other instructor was Chief Radioman Dorman Chauncey. He also had learned on his own and conducted intercept at the U.S. Navy sites in Hawaii and Peking. By 1941 they had graduated 176 kana operators. Of course these 176 radio operators went back to the intercept sites and/or sea and trained others. The first assignment of each morning was to climb a ladder to the roof of a concrete blockhouse where the classes took place, in great secrecy, atop the sixth wing of the old Navy Department Building. The building is gone now but it was about where the Vietnam Memorial stands. Among themselves Op-20-G graduates were the "On The Roof Gang."

In addition to the communications intelligence center (COMINT) at Op-20-G operated by Miss Aggie, Safford set up two additional COMINT centers. One at Pearl Harbor called HYPO (the word for the ship's flagman's H), aka the Dungeon and one in the famous tunnel at Corregidor where

General MacArthur's headquarters was before he was run out of the Philippine Islands and his men sent on the notorious Baton Death March. The later was moved to Australia when MacArthur left.

The intercept sites for listening post and direction-finding were: The US embassy in Shanghai, China until about 1935; Guam until December 1941; Olongapo City in the Philippine Islands; and Astoria on the Oregon coast. Some intercept was conducted aboard ships, principally the USS Augusta and the USS Gold Star.

I used to listen to the war stories and reminiscing of the old NCOs (Sergeants in the Marines and Army and Chief Petty Officer, or just Chiefs in the Navy) at the "rocker clubs" in the area or as civilians at Arlington Hall Station where the Armed Forces Security Service was collectively after World War II. Usually the fist of the ship's telegraphers was very crisp, exact, and beautiful. They took their job as seriously as a violinist in a symphony orchestra. Like a violinist the operators—Japanese and Americans alike—bought their own key. The key was called a bug. Go to www.google.com and search for telegraph key if you want to hear one. The old navy chiefs had names for the operators to whom they listened a lot. Names like the "Hornpiper," "Waltzing Moose," "Skip to Me Glue," "Speedy Gonzales," Yokahama Mama," and "Rubber Atoll" whose ship hung around the Atolls. One that made a big difference in the Battle of Midway was Super Smootho (named for a dressing sailors used on razor straps). That was Admiral Yamamoto's chief operator; he was Admiral of the whole Japanese Fleet.

So let's take a look at the situation post 1930:

- Traffic analysis had established the location and identification of each Japanese ship in the Pacific to within 100 miles or less. This was easier than you might think because direction-finding gave the location of both the ship to whom the signal is sent and the transmitting ship (or port). Unlike mail and casual radio, a message could not be one way. The sender had to have acknowledgment that a strong signal was being received. If one has to repeat the signal, it has to be re-encrypted, not good.

- Radio operators could identify the fist of most clerks so the ship was identified.

- Message preamble could usually identify the hierarchy to establish the "order of battle."

The flying clipper boats had passenger roots that landed at the Comint and receiver sites. The crews of these planes were mostly reserve naval officers who had a strong-box in the nose of the plane. Intercept data would be passed around the Pacific and registered mail would be sent to D.C. from the West Coast.

One of the first successes was from the station at Corregidor. They notified the Navy Department that the Japanese Navy was on maneuvers and was preparing to land in Manchuria, and gave a detailed order-of-battle. This was done almost entirely by traffic analysis and direction-finding. It got Washington's attention. There was more to this COMINT than what had previously met their eye. In addition the additives for the Red Book had almost completely been established so some actual messages could be shown to the Navy Department.

The Japanese replaced the Red Book with a more sophisticated code on December 1, 1930. However, the new code, called Blue, contained numeric patterns that so closely resembled Red that Driscoll and her teams were able to decipher and translate Blue in only two years. And so from 1932 to July 1, 1939, there was a hey-day of both traffic analysis and reading the Imperial Navy's traffic. This was the time of "Hoovervilles," soup kitchens, and preoccupation with things other than an attack by Japan on the United States. If anyone had asked either a man standing in a soup-line or an admiral, "Do you think Japan would attack the United States?," he would probably have laughed and asked, "Which state?"

During this time the officer corps was relatively small. The navy was unique as a military branch in that all officers had to do at least half-time sea duty, usually every three years, never on the same ship twice. Unlike army officers, these men lived together in tight quarters. So the navy officer's corps was much like a big family. One of the consequences was that the Op-20-G got to know who would be interested in studying language, radio, cryptography, and related duties. As a result, there were a few dozen officers and enlisted men who played a key role in our story of the Japanese JN-25 code work from 1939 on throughout World War II. Of course the number exploded after mid 1942. On July 1, 1939 JN-25 was introduced. Of the three analysis centers, Miss Aggie's at Op-20-G and the Australian Station took on JN-25 until war broke out. HYPO (aka the Dungeon) at Pearl worked on a special 'flag ship' code. In 17 months, starting from scratch, they had mastered JN-25. But the Japanese changed the additive book on December 1, 1941, just before the War. The HYPO group jumped in also on JN-25 after the War started on December 7, 1941 and they were far enough along in additive recovery and with traffic analysis and some tricks, by March 1942 to change the tides of war at the Battle of Midway.

We need to go into some detail about how additive book entries are established. This is important because only with this understanding can you really appreciate the advantages of public key cryptography that is used today.

There were 33,000 code groups, "words" in the code book, and 300 pages with 100 random numbers on each page for the additive book. There were also some traditions, or unique characteristics, in the code book that helps so much. One might think, as the creators of the Japanese codes did, that adding a random number to a code "word" would make the transmitted message a random number which would befuddle any attack. Two conventions of JN-25 (and previous books) that immensely facilitated the attack were:

(1) The sum of the digits in any of the five digit code entries had to add up to be divisible evenly by 3. Example: the number for "anchor" was 32976. 3+2+9+7+6=27 and 27 is evenly divisible by 3. This was used as a garble check. After the message was written out, the clerk had to add the digits to make sure he had not copied them down wrong. Of all the numbers between 00102 and 99999, every third one is divisible by 3, e.g., 00105, 00108, 00111, . . . and so on.

(2) The code for numbers were 00000 is 0, 00102 is 1, 00306 is 3, 00408 is 4, 00510 is 5, 00612 is 6, 00714 is 7, 00816 is 8, and 00918 is 9.

Now let's suppose that a message comes in and we know some numbers that will be sent in the preamble. We can make a good guess from traffic analysis, direction-finding, and fist characteristics. We subtract these numbers from the message and get, say, a dozen additives in a row, we think. We take these dozen additives and subtract them from thousands of messages. If we are lucky we will find a string of resulting numbers in a row that have sums evenly divisible by 3. What is the probability of this happening? If you flip a coin and get 6 heads straight in a row, the chance of this happening is $(1/2)(1/2)(1/2)(1/2)(1/2)(1/2)=1/64$. This will happen one time in 64 tries. Similarly, 1/3 of our possible numbers will be evenly divisible by 3. So the chances of getting 6 in a row when subtracting our trial additives is $(1/3)(1/3)(1/3)(1/3)(1/3)(1/3)=1/729$. This would happen by chance only one time in 729. We take these 6 code numbers, make a guess at the

meaning and store them in our (temporary) code book. There
were no computers but there was a machine that was better
than anything they could have imagined a few years earlier.
When we get into our story, Commander Joe Rochefort, director for COMINT at HYPO in Pearl Harbor, will be walking
around all day in the Dungeon with a loose old dinner jacket
over his khaki uniform so he has lots of pockets for IBM cards.
If you offered Commander Rochefort 5,000 good men for one
of his IBM sorting machines, he would have turned you down.

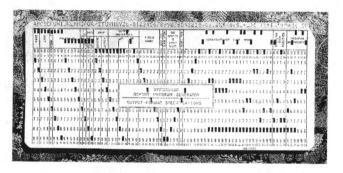

*Figure 1.7. IBM card used in sorting machines. Notice that
the rows go from 0 to 9 from top to bottom.*

If you never saw an IBM card, by the way, they were the
size of a dollar bill made of cardboard about the stiffness of
a birthday card. There was a matrix of holes so they could
be carried on cog wheels or conveyer belts. The cards were
covered with a grid of 1mm x 3mm printed boxes where the
punch machine would punch holes to designate numbers.
You had a paper punch to manually punch holes in the places
where marked rectangles were. The cleverness of the IBM
cards was that you could get a print-out of any assortment
that you wished. Like playing the card game "Go Fish." Give
me all your 2s? I don't have any; Go fish.

One thing to remember about this type of system is that once you get a toe-hold, a few additives and a few code groups, with traffic analysis and knowledge of previous "habits," identical messages encrypted twice and sent to two places, and stringent protocols, the attack can grow rapidly. Luckily, the Japanese thought the system would be secure if the additive book was periodically changed. It would have been a logistic nightmare to change the code book and the additive book at the same time on thousands of ships and hundreds of shore bases.

A shameful thing happened after Pearl Harbor. The Navy Department canned Admiral Husband Kimmel for allowing the catastrophe to happen. Investigations years later showed that the Navy Department was the culprit; they withheld information that the attack was imminent. The nation's good luck was that he was replaced by the brilliant Admiral Chester W. Nimitz. The first brilliant thing he did was to reassure the existing Pacific Fleet staff that he had confidence in them and wanted them to continue. His Intelligence Officer, Lt. Commander Edwin Layton, was a good friend and colleague of six or seven of the "Of The Roof Gang" in the Dungeon at HYPO during the 1930s. Lieutenant Safford had just assigned four officers to HYPO who were recent graduates of the language school in Tokyo and also graduates of Miss Aggie's crypto school at Op-20-G. Another lucky break was that the USS Tennessee was sunk on December 7, freeing Lt. Commander Joseph Finnegan, a crypto junkie, a graduate of the language school in Tokyo and Op-20-G. Another lucky break was the USS California was at the bottom of Pearl Harbor with all the musical instruments of the ship's band. They were trying to retrieve their instruments when Eddie Layton sent them all to the Dungeon to work. They were the organizers of the IBM machines and many of them turned out to be cryptanalysis *par excellence* and went on to brilliant careers at National Security Agency after the War.

I cannot stress too much that this was a very, very unusual military situation. For example, five of the HYPO gang, including Commander Joseph Rochefort the honcho of HYPO and Eddie Layton served together on the USS Pennsylvania during the 1930s. Eddie Layton was assigned to the US Ambassador's staff in Tokyo in addition to going to the language school there. He knew most of the HYPO gang from that duty. And Joe Rochefort took over command of Op-20-G in 1936, relieving Commander Safford for his (compulsory) sea duty. The language school in Tokyo closed in the fall of 1941 and the last five students, Lieutenants Gilvan M. Slonim, Forrest R. Biard, John G. Roenigk, Arthur L. Benedict, and John R. Bromley, barely caught a freighter to Shanghai and then on to Pearl just before the war started. All but Forrest Biard were wrenched from the HYPO Dungeon to listen to telephone wire taps. To hear Forrest Biard tell it, the four who contributed the most to our success at the Battle of Midway were Joe Rochefort (one of the three who started Op-20-G) who, with Eddie Layton spoke un-accented Japanese, although they both learned it as adults in Tokyo from 1929 to 1932. That in itself is an incredible feat.

Eddie Layton was a personal friend of Admiral Yamamoto, the director of the whole Japanese fleet until he was shot down in 1943 on an inspection tour as the result of a famous message decryption. As Admiral Nimitz's intelligence officer, Eddie Layton was the digester and sales representative for the Dungeon. Tommy Dyer was Rochefort's second in command. Tommy Finnegan mentioned above was next in line but you could only get about half of the group to agree with this; they would otherwise put Tommy Dyer one notch up for group coordination. Both these men had incredible linguistic, crypto, traffic analysis skills and work ethic. It is not quite fair because Tommy Finnegan had an appendage. Tommy Finnegan's desk and surrounding tables were filled with random stacks of IBM print-outs, apple cores, coffee cups, IBM cards, cigarette butts, reports that were due in right now. Major Alva B. (Red) Lasswell, USMC, and Tommy worked as a team. Red Lasswell had neat piles of only what he was working on at present sitting on a polished oak desk. He was Mister Organized himself.

Tommy had so many brain circuits going at once that sometimes they ignited. Major Lasswell would take matters in hand to get the job done. Finnegan had all these hunches based on (what seemed to be) nothing. He was usually right. Tommy Dyer had a work-mate too, Lt. Commander Wesley A. (Ham) Wright. He, among other things, just before the Midway attack, came up with the decipherment of the date and time designator for the actual planned day of the Japanese attack. And of course, Lt. Biard, one of the best linguists and synthesizers left himself off the list out of modesty. In reality there was no one who contributed more than others. For example, there was the team of Lieutenant Commander John A. Huckins and Lieutenant John A. Williams, who put together the traffic analysis picture that would have gone a long way to showing the Japanese intentions without a word of message translation, as was successfully done by the enlisted men at Station Corregidor in 1930. And remember, Rochefort would not trade an IBM machine for 5000 men. Well, the machines were set up by Lt. Commander Jack S. Holtwich. And don't discount Lt. Commander Allyn Cole, a linguist with extensive experience on Corregidor. In January, Barney Calhoun and Philip Leigh joined the cipher and traffic sections respectively to give fresh inputs. And there was Lieutenant W. Jasper Holmes, a professor of engineering at the

University of Hawaii. He graduated from Annapolis in 1918 (along with Captain Joseph Safford, creator of Op-20-G) and retired in 1936. Recalled to duty, it was he who had the brilliant idea of having Midway send the fake message regarding their shortage of fresh water. Our decryption of the Japanese response to this message synched Midway as the identity of the onslaught.

There were about thirty sailors who punched IBM cards and kept the place ship-shape as much as possible. From December 7, 1941, to June 8, 1942, there were no musters, no keeping track of work hours, no uniform-of-the-day, no schedules other than Commander Rochefort submitting a status report every morning to Lieutenant Layton. Someone described it as like a submarine under attack from depth charges. They all lived on sandwiches, coffee and pep pills sitting around in bowls all over the place; occasionally going up for a good meal, a night's sleep and a bath, and a fresh uniform.

By April 15, 1942, the additive book of JN-25 was at least half recovered. It was not until March 15 that the plan for the attack on Midway was solidified by the Japanese high command. The final decision was a result of General Jimmy Doolittle's bomber attack on Tokyo; controlling the mid Pacific was more important than island hopping near Australia. The battle plan was to:

- Send a seaplane to Hawaii on about May 28 for a quick bombing raid as a disguise for checking to make sure the two carriers, *Hornet* and *Enterprise*, were not going to be near Midway. This had been done once before. They thought the US had only two carriers. They sunk the *Lexington* in the Coral Sea and they thought they had sunk the *Yorktown*, but they had not.

- Put a chain of submarines between Hawaii and Midway to attack the US Navy rescue operation for Midway after it was struck and/or occupied.

- Send an attacking force of two carriers and associated armada to invade the Alaskan Aleutian Islands on June 3 as a diversion from the June 4 attack on Midway.

On June 4 bring a strike force (*Kido Butai*, a Japanese carrier type armada) of four carriers, sundry destroyers, and two battlewagons, within 100 miles of Midway to destroy air fields and planes and soften up Midway. The carriers were *Kaga*, *Akagi*, *Soryu*, and *Hiryu*.

Invade on June 5 with landing crafts of three groups of about 5000 soldiers supported with off-shore heavy artillery from the invasion force.

Admiral Yamamoto on his flag ship Yamato and an extensive armada were to sit out 300 miles ready to attack the US Navy as they were forced to come to the rescue of Midway.

Radio silence all the way around until the attack.

Admiral Nimitz had three carriers, *Enterprise*, *Hornet*, and *Yorktown*, with the *Lexington* having been sunk off the Coral Sea a month before. Most other capital ships were sunk at Pearl Harbor. The US carriers had been out to sea when Pearl Harbor was attacked. The Japanese thought the *Yorktown* was also sunk but it limped home just in time and was miraculously patched up in a week—another group of sailors besides those in the Dungeon who worked like crazy in the last few weeks before the Midway attack.

Admiral Nimitz had all this information by May 20. Had you been Admiral Nimitz, what plan would you make? First off there were skeptics, some with political motives, even in Naval Operations (e.g., Captain Redman who was to take over Op-20-G). In addition, conformation was absolutely necessary because any plan would require all of Pacific Fleet resources and that would leave all other US possessions vulnerable. So he asked HYPO for proof. He got definite proof of where and when. The "where" came from University of Hawaii engineering professor turned traffic analyst, Lt. Commander Jasper Holmes. He had been involved with the installation of a water distillery at Midway for fresh water generation.

I forgot to say, one of the best weapons Admiral Nimitz had was an underwater cable to Midway. Orders were given to Midway to notify Pacific Fleet Headquarters in plain text that Midway had only two weeks of fresh water supply. Sure enough, the Japanese invasion force quartermaster request- ed an additional water tanker because there was only a two week supply of fresh water on AF (●— ●●—●) the Midway designate, established in early March by Rochefort. This was proof of the "where." Thanks to Lieutenant Finnegan, who dug through old decrypts for the solid month of April, the "when" was also found. He and Lasswell found the date-time code book entries pattern in mid-May. It was a matrix of the kana,

sa	a i u e o ka ki ku ke ko ra ri ru re ro ta chi tsu te to n ma mi mu me mo ha hi fu he ho
si	i u e o ka ki ku ke ko ra ri ru re ro ta chi tsu te to n ma mi mu me mo ha hi fu he ho a
su	u e o ka ki ku ke ko ra ri ru re ro ta chi tsu te to n ma mi mu me mo ha hi fu he ho a i
se	e o ka ki ku ke ko ra ri ru re ro ta chi tsu te to n ma mi mu me mo ha hi fu he ho a i u
so	o ka ki ku ke ko ra ri ru re ro ta chi tsu te to n ma mi mu me mo ha hi fu he ho a i ue e
ta	ka ki ku ke ko ra ri ru re ro ta chi tsu te to n ma mi mu me mo ha hi fu he ho a i u o
ti	ki ku ke ko ra ri ru re ro ta chi tsu te to n ma mi mu me mo ha hi fu he ho a i u o ka
tu	ku ke ko ra ri ru re ro ta chi tsu te to n ma mi mu me mo ha hi fu he ho a i u o ka ki
te	ke ko ra ri ru re ro ta chi tsu te to n ma mi mu me mo ha hi fu he ho a i u o ka ki ku

to	ko ra ri ru re ro ta chi tsu te to n ma mi mu me mo ha hi fu he ho a i u o ka ki ku ke
na	ra ri ru re ro ta chi tsu te to n ma mi mu me mo ha hi fu he ho a i u o ka ki ku ke ko
ni	ri ru re ro ta chi tsu te to n ma mi mu me mo ha hi fu he ho a i u o ka ki ku ke ko ra

Figure 1.7. The date-time code used in JN-25. June 4 would be ta ke ko. The ko was for a garble check.

This was the plan drawn up by Nimitz's staff:

- Bring the fleet into Pearl Harbor, refurbish, repair, refuel, rearm and be ready to sail before the Japanese reconnaissance plane came in, on or about May 28.

- Thwart the reconnaissance plane's mission by having a deterrent at the Frigate Shoal, the place where the plane had to rendezvous with a Japanese submarine for refueling. These details were known from decrypts.

- Get the US fleet out of Pearl and beyond the ring of submarines of item 2 in the Japanese plan.

- Move as many torpedo planes, dive bombers, fighters, PT Boats, PBY scout pontoon planes, and B17 high altitude bombers to Midway and be ready by June 1. When the *Kaga*, *Akagi*, *Soryu*, and *Hiryu* came to "soften up Midway" and destroy the planes there, the Midway planes would be off to attack the carriers. Keep in mind that even fragile little bi-planes of World War I vintage could sink capital ships as a dive bomber or torpedo plane. That is, any capital ship that did not have fighter planes to protect it. However, carriers were still very vulnerable to other capital ships at night.

- When the planes from the *Kaga*, *Akagi*, *Soryu*, and *Hiryu* returned and were rearming and refueling, the torpedo planes and dive bombers from the *Enterprise*, *Hornet*, and *Yorktown* would strike.

- Bring troops to Midway and dig in for the invasion.

The Battle of Midway proceeded on June 4, 1942, as follows:

5:53 am   Japanese formation spotted 93 miles from Midway. This was about half of the planes of the *Kido Butai*'s carriers *Kaga, Akagi, Soryu,* and *Hiryu*.

6:04 am   74 miles away. All Midway planes scrambled.

6:12 am   Twelve F4F fighters attack the formation before they come in.

6:31 am   All guns open up on Midway, including handguns of all the 3000 soldiers brought in to fight the invasion.

7:00 am   Japanese planes start the (about 2-hour) return to the carriers, with a message saying, we need a second attack because no planes were on the ground at Midway.

7:05 am   Midway planes attack the carriers with minimal success.

7:15 am   Admiral Nagumo, commander of the *Kido Butai*, orders switching from torpedoes to bombs for the remaining half of the attack planes on the *Kido Butai*.

7:28 am   *Kido Butai* scout plane spots ten US ships 150 miles away. He does not see any US carriers (yet).

7:45 am   Admiral Nagumo of the *Kido Butai* reverses order for second Midway attack and to switch torpedoes back on attack planes.

8:20   Scout plane sends message that there is one US Carrier bringing up the rear.

8:20 am   Midway planes make a second attack on the *Kido Butai*. Very little damage done but Japanese fighters must refuel.

8:30 am   Admiral Nagumo orders returning planes from Midway to land on carriers.

9:18 am   Torpedo planes from *Enterprise* and *Yorktown* attack *Kido Butai*. Torpedo planes annihilated by Japanese fighters.

10:25 am   All four *Kido Butai* carriers are "sitting ducks" for the dive bombers of the US carriers that just arrived.

10:30 am   In five minutes the *Kaga*, *Akagi*, and *Soryu* are destroyed.

1:30 pm   The planes of the remaining carrier, *Hiryu*, attack the *Yorktown* and fatally wound it. Most of the Japanese attacking planes are lost. The *Yorktown* was finally sunk the next day by a Japanese submarine. *Yorktown* suffers minimal loss of planes or sailors.

5:30 pm   The *Hiryu* is sunk by the dive bombers of the *Enterprise* and *Hornet*.

June 5, 1942, Admiral Yamamoto breaks radio silence and calls off the invasion of Midway. Radio and direction-finding operators note, "Super Smootho got transferred or Admiral Yamamoto has his fleet out there"—ready to pounce. (Not surprisingly, Super Smootho, Yamamoto's chief telegrapher, had the "most beautiful fist" in the Navy.) Direction-finding pinned Yamamoto to about 200 miles from the *Kido Butai*. As a result the US task force lay low to avoid a fight.

End of story, end of Japanese domination in the Pacific.

But Midway was also one of these moments that concentrate forces of history, that in one intense burst crystallize what might have otherwise taken years to coalesce from the fog of events. Midway decisively announced the end of the age of the battleship. The battleship's brawn was simply no match for the long reach of the carrier. Of even further-reaching consequence, the American victory at Midway moved code breaking and signals intelligence from an arcane, little-understood, and usually unappreciated specialty to the very center of military operations.[8]

Top-drawer analysis of Midway by the Japanese fleet command concluded that they:

- Should have had a more intensive submarine ring around Pearl Harbor to engage the US fleet whenever it would sail.

- Could have easily used twice as many carriers and would have never been caught with their planes/pants down.

- They relied too heavily of their prediction of what the US forces would do.

- They did not consider that the US forces would know exactly what they had planned, down to the last detail.

Yet you cannot really fault the Japanese. All nations cut their crypto teeth during World War II. The US crypto machines were routinely broken by the Germans. Very few people know that; it was only reveled recently.[9]

Ditto on the other side. The British broke the Enigma. Only the Italians were savvy enough to do crypto properly. Nobody broke their ciphers. They had a system very similar to that of the Japanese. They did what the Japanese should have done: instead of an additive book that they changed periodically, they had an "additive page" for every day of the month/year and used it only once. The Japanese could have easily done this logistically. They could have sent out the date-time code and that would be associated with an additive page that was never used again.

---

[8] *Battle of Wits*, Stephen Budiansky, Touchstone, page 21.
[9] http://seclists.org/fulldisclosure/2004/Oct/287.

This is an important point to get across. Indeed, it is my main reason to include the Battle of Midway in this narrative. Take for example a message intercepted by Op-20-G in which the context of the message is known. They could strip off all the additives. So what? They would never be used again and the context of the message is already known. Well actually, they could be used again but not in any predictable pattern; if the list of numerals is truly random they can come up again, but not in a predictable way. Another way of saying this is that the additive book is not random numerals; it is a repeatable sequence of numerals used over and over.

By the way, in modern crypto, the random set of numerals, called the session key, is sent along with the message in a way (RSA algorithm) that cannot be discerned. Non-mathematician baby-boomers have a gut feeling that with enough effort messages can be deciphered. They get this misunderstanding from the 1942–1990 era history through which they have lived.

CHAPTER 2. THE BIRTH OF THE NSA

Army Security Agency

April Fool's Day, 1952. I sat down on a stone wall. A retainer wall for the dugout road behind the Science Hall at Fairmont State College just 20 miles from where I went to high school in Grafton, West Virginia. It was a half-hour before partial differential equations class and nothing to do. Senior year was mostly classes in math or electives, so no worry about finals or anything. Then it hit me. The rest of life is a breeze! I jumped off the wall and did a little clog step. No more money needed. Worst case, I can just stay at home and have plenty of food, clothing, and shelter and have time on my hands to enjoy life. No more keeping my eye out for good but cheap clothes. No more getting up early to press my wool pants and iron my shirt. No more asking for summer jobs or asking girls out. You ask fifty times and forty-nine look down their noses and say, "no." Not, "gee, I would, but..." or "that's nice, but"; just "no." I can go home and get younger girls; they usually like older guys and you don't have to spend money with them if you don't have any.

You would think I would have thought earlier about what would happen next, after graduating, but I had not, at least not in the particular. Work wouldn't really be work anymore. When I was seven, I went door to door selling the *Saturday Evening Post*. When I was eight, I graduated to the *Ladies Home Journal*. I never did get any money because I could not keep the money straight. This man came around in a big fancy car and collected the money. Magazines were a nickel. So if he gave me ten, I sold seven. Had to give him 4 cents for at least eight. Always lost track of one or two. I wanted to get out of that door-to-door stuff in the worst way. "Want to buy a *Saturday Evening Post*?" "I told you yesterday, kid, quit coming around here with those *** *Saturday Evening Posts*." Then it was the Grit. Then the glory days of a real paper route. So I thought. Always someone who said, "I'll pay next week, kid." I knew he wouldn't. So I cut down from 35 to 34 and skipped him. "Mr. Jumjagger called and said you skipped him, did not deliver his paper," the editor said. "He didn't pay last week." "He'll pay, deliver."

I had red cards about the size of a dollar bill on a ring for each customer. The dates were around the edge. When they paid, I punched out the date with a hole puncher. A bag, a hole puncher, and a ring of cards were the stock and trade of a paper boy. I had lots of problems. One was that about two thirds paid on time. But the newspaper made the delivery boys pay at the window when they got their papers. I aspired to be a paperboy because that was what the big boys did. Little did I know that I would lose more than I did on *The Saturday Evening Post* and that I would have to get jobs cutting grass to pay the difference. Another problem was that I would sing, whistle and daydream and walk right by customers. Especially after a movie, with arias like 'Ole Man River' and 'People Will Say We're In Love.' Then there was this crazy kid that wanted to trade me my paper route for a job inside the newspaper office. All you had to do was print addresses off these dog-tag-looking things that ran through a machine and printed addresses on a half sheet of paper. You rolled a newspaper into the half sheet and glued it. You carried a canvas mailbag, bigger than you were, to the depot for the train. Cold hard cash, even if I made mistakes. A step up was my next job of delivering groceries in a wagon for a mom-and-pop grocery store. That was cold hard work, but fun. Some customers were two or three miles from the store but I got to go in their kitchens. Sometimes they gave me cake and pie. Mostly these housewives wanted someone to talk to. The way I saw it, I got paid just to be their friend. It would have been a perfect joy had they let me tune the radio off the stupid drug-store-cowboy music and onto some Broadway stuff or folk music by local performers.

Jobs got easier: janitor in a local movie house, stock boy in a clothing store. Then graduated to a sporting goods store where I could talk to all the hunters and fishermen. Cutting a right-of-way for the power company in college—that was hard physical work but fun; much like it is fun to play ball but hard physical work. Then a plush job in my senior year as a boat dock attendant and life guard on the Tygart Lake and Saturdays delivering groceries in a real truck. What I hated about all this was asking for 50 jobs and finally getting one.

On that April fool's Day 1952, sitting on the wall, it dawned on me; no more asking 50 people for a job this summer! Maybe I could get paid for doing what I did anyhow, for nothing—making radios and antennas, or antennae as they still said then. Maybe I could get paid for moving up the spectrum to microwave. That started a long climb up the spectrum to heterodyne radios of one-one hundredth of a millimeter wavelength where the smallest hair is a long wave antenna.

I'd built my first antenna years ago; it was a 40 meters wavelength. This was my second year in high school and the boys were coming home from the war. One teacher was Lieutenant, JG Lynn Faulkner, just out of the Navy. Later I found out that he had worked at the MIT Radiation Laboratory— the US contribution to radar, catching up with the famed radar home-chain along the White Cliffs of Dover during the 1940 Battle of Britain. I worked there later myself when it was part of MIT. He knew everything. He showed us how to build radios from scratch, even blow glass for homemade vacuum tubes. In my own little world, I thought everyone knew math. I went to trigonometry class like a feminist in the 70s went to a consciousness-raising meeting. Just to share exciting things that they all knew about. No one told me you were supposed to wait until you went to class to learn it. No one told me, either, that you had to learn to read and write to graduate from high school. One afternoon I bugged out of class and went to the diner down the street. I was in a booth enjoying a cup of coffee and a cigarette. Oh, my gosh. Mr. Clayton (aka Shorty), the principal, was in a booth doing the same thing. He was too short for me to see over the booth, so I missed him. I always had a job, so I had money for cigarettes and coffee. As he got up to pay the cashier, he saw me (not my cigarette; I slipped it to the floor). He said, "Nelson, what will you ever do when you get out of school?"

I said, "Be a mathematician." He didn't say "You're truant," "you shouldn't be here," or anything. He just stared at me for a while and then walked out. Again I thought, "I'm in for it now." And I was.

That afternoon after school in our radio room, Mr. Faulkner told me. "You are not going to graduate. Miss Batten [the English teacher] told me you could not read and write, is that right?" "No, that's not right."

"Then tell me what that says." He pointed to some words. I faked reading, "Yes sir, I can read and write, that says the imaginary part of the impedance shows the phase relationship." "Which word is impedance and which word is imaginary?" "Well, it wouldn't say the impedance part of the imaginary." The next day Miss Batten stuck the script of a play, *Dear Ruth*, in my hand and said, "You have the lead part. Have Act One memorized by this weekend."

Now I was in deep trouble. We lived in a large three-story old wood house. No furnace. In the downstairs parlor there was a coal-burning grate. That put out a lot of heat, but the bedrooms were cold. The four boys, Roger, Jim, Dick, and me, had the biggest bedroom and it had a gas fireplace. Our bedroom was the only cozy place in the house in winter except for the parlor and kitchen. When I was a senior, Dick was a freshman. He was the pride of the whole family. He took operatic voice lessons every Saturday in Clarksburg, about 20 miles away. He sang at weddings, church services, school assemblies, and in the shower after football practice. Clarksburg was more than half Italian immigrants; they put on an Italian Opera at least once a year. So he (and after a while I) loved classical music, and Broadway shows that were popular in the movies during those days. One just could not get classical music, especially in the back hills of West Virginia. Radio, as popular as it was, was only local, about a 50 mile radius. It was not local for me. The only time I had to listen to that drug-store-cowboy trash music was when I went into kitchens to deliver groceries. I designed a rhombic antenna. A rhombic is a highly directional, high gain, antenna formed from four wires, long compared to a wave length, formed into a diamond shape. Twin wires with a certain spacing and size go to the radio as a transmission line. We pointed it northeast toward New York City. Chicago and New York had the only classical music stations in the East. On sub-freezing winter nights Dick and I were by our gas stove that was built into the wall, drinking tea and listening to 1650 kilohertz on the AM dial. WQXR from New York City. They are still a co-sponsor of the Metropolitan Opera Saturday broadcasts.

So this was the background one evening when I came home with the script to *Dear Ruth*. "Dick, what is this word: s-i-t-u-a-t-i-o-n?", I spelled. "You don't know what that word is?" "If I did, I wouldn't ask," I said.

"Look it up in the dictionary." "That's crazy," I said. "Why? He asked. "That's about the stupidest thing I ever heard anyone say." "Why"? I insisted. OK," I found it in the dictionary and pointed to it. "I got it right here in the dictionary," (Webster's Collegiate Dictionary 1936): sit'u-a'tion (-a ' shûn), n, 1. Manner in which an object is placed; location; also, a locality. 2." I say to Dick, jabbing my finger to the word in the dictionary. "I'm looking at it; that doesn't tell me how to say the word." "Now read that and tell me what 'sisen' (trying to pronounce it) means; go ahead, read to me what it means." Dick reads, "Manner in which an object is placed." "OK, that just tells me everything about 'sisen', doesn't it?" I raved like a preacher.

"How to say it and what it means? I'm gonna put my fist down easy, I'm 'sisen' it? Now I'm going to slam it down and bust it, is that 'sisen' it? That is exactly what everyone says to me if I ask them how to say a written word, look it up in the dictionary." "OK, I'll read it to you," Dick said. Next evening, same thing. Next evening, same thing. "I'm not reading to you anymore. I'm sick and tired of spending my evenings reading that stupid play over and over."

"But I can read it myself now, the first four pages. Listen to this." "I don't want to listen to that. I'm sick of that." I went up the third floor balcony and started taking apart the matching network for the rhombic antenna. "You can't do that," Dick said. He was beside himself. "All I need is two more nights and Act I will be finished."

That is how I learned to read.

The play was a smash. I was a smash and graduated from high school. Four years later, in 1952, I was sitting at home on the balcony by my rhombic antenna transmission line. My revelation while sitting on the Science Hall wall a few weeks before on April Fool's Day where this story starts, had come true. I could go down to the YMCA and shoot pool or play ball. I could take a boat and row for hundreds of miles in the Tygart Lake without seeing a house, if I wanted to. Lots of high-school-age girls liked hanging around older college boys. I had a pile of books that were too time-consuming to have enjoyed during college. I could read them now. I heard someone downstairs and went down. "Hi, Uncle Joe" — my uncle Joe Ondo. My mother had 12 brothers and sisters, so I had lots of uncles. He was our mailman. "You got a letter from the draft board." He knew all about the draft. He still has a yellow tint from a bad case of malaria in the South Pacific. "You open it," I said. "I'm not allowed to open people's mail. What does it say?" handing me the letter. "It says my four year deferment for college is over and I have to report for induction. I got books I want to read. The guys they want me to go over there and kill; they got books they want to read, too."

"You got to go, you know that." "OK Uncle Joe, you make the choice. (1) I go and get killed and Korea is free for democracy. (2) I don't go and get to live my life and the Communists rule all of Korea. Which do you choose?" "I can't choose that."

"Of course you can. Let me put it another way. Suppose a telegram came to my mother saying, we regret to inform you that your son, Nelson, has ......bla bla." I drape a blanket from the couch over my head like an Arab and say, "And the Lord came down and tapped you on the shoulder and said, Joe, we can get that boy back if you are willing to approve me giving Korea to the Chinese. What is your answer?"

"It doesn't make any difference, you got to go. That's not the real choice. The real choice is either you go to jail or take a risk of not coming back; which is pretty small. You're going to be making choices all your life between taking one risk or another. What happens in Korea has nothing to do with it. This isn't even important enough to be declared a war, so no one really cares much what the outcome is."

So down to the post office I went.

"Hi Serg."

"Hi Nelson, let's go get a hotdog."

He always tried to bribe recruits with hotdogs, so he was a potbellied recruiting sergeant; and he always did his homework and knew who was up for the draft.

"You been fishing?"

"No, I'm going to take a sack of grub and a boat and stay out on the lake for a few days. I've got lots of time and don't have a job." There is this cave with a hangover, you pull your boat under the hangover and the cave mouth is just four feet above the water line. There are rocks that make steps up to the cave. The water drips constantly from a place in the roof of the cave about 10 feet in from the mouth. Someone has put a big bolder with a basin under the drip and there you have a basin of clean water all the time, summer and winter. The best time is when it is raining. You can set a trotline to get your fish, have a cook fire next to the water basin. Just bring a few candles and snooze during the rain and do what you want.

"You don't have all that much time; the draft will get you," the Sergeant said.

"How'd you know that?"

"I know everything about all the draftees."

"You like killing people, Serg?"

"No, why would you ask a question like that?"

"That's your job. That's what George Patton used to say, the job of a solder is to kill people as fast as he can. I'm not like you; I don't want to kill people."

"I don't want to kill people, either; I'm not like you either. I don't have a big house with a mom and dad that both work and a college degree, and I can't loaf around up the lake. You're a college boy. You ought to know what Charles Dickens said: only rich people can afford high morals."

"Thanks for the hotdog and Coke, Serg," starting to get up from the booth.

"Wait a minute, wait a minute. I might have what you are looking for. We just got this good deal for college graduates or anyone with two years of college who can pass a certain test. If they've specialized in electronics or languages or math, they can join this new branch of the Army called ASA."

"Do I have to kill people?" I said.

"This branch of the Army broke off from the Signal Corps. It has to do with coded messages, I've been told, but I'm not supposed to give that information out to recruits."

"You just did."

"Like Charles Dickens said, I got to meet my quota."

"If I join up, I'll have to join for four years. My two brothers had to join the Navy for four years."

"No no, you can join for three years."

"Why only three years?"

"I don't know; I don't run the Army. Maybe they need people bad."

I took my bag of grub, candles, books, a boat and a trot-line and went out to my cave. I only stayed a few days. I guess I was the original hyperactive kid; I get bored real fast.

Joining ASA was probably a good choice because, as you will see, I was involved in the setting up of the new federal agency, the NSA, decreed by Congress in 1952. In addition, most of the third year, I was allowed TDY (temporary duty) to go to graduate school, free from any Army duties at a full Sergeant's salary. After my tour was up, I went on to gradu-ate school on the GI bill, consulting for the NSA at times, and then right back into the NSA.

The summer of 1952 went fast. Basic training was a breeze. I was called in and asked if I wanted to go to OCS (Officers Training School). It meant signing up for another year. Four years, no way. It took all the will power I had to not do it. Not because I wanted to; I didn't want to. I wanted to do it just to spite my dad. I went home in the middle of my basic training to my grandfather, Bruce McIntosh's, funeral. What a donny-brook. My uncles Benny, Havard, Harry, Arthur, Jay, Willard, McIntosh, all my mother's brothers went to town and looked up a couple of West Virginia State Troopers and wanted to fight. The Troopers said no thanks, so they just fought among themselves. My uncles looked like the typical log thrower in the Scottish games—sandy haired brutes. My dad and some others were with them too. When my dad was drunk, he al-ways vented what had been bothering him lately, be it the "robber barons" or the racists or some individual. That day it was me. He was upset that I would choose to go to OCS. When I told him I had that option, he raved, "You have no business being an officer." "Why?" I said in surprise. "You just don't have any business." "Well, that's no answer."

"You can't hear out of one ear and you can't see out of one eye and an officer has to take responsibility for his men; and you can't do that." No one knew I had those maladies outside the family and I resented him trying to restrict my life because of them, as he always did. It was easy for me to cheat on physical examinations. But I knew that his real resentment had been brewing for years because I had stopped him from abusing my mother when he was drunk. I turned down OCS because I did not want to increase the probability of having to kill people. I had better chances of not having to do that in ASA. I suppose at heart I was a conscientious objector.

It had nothing to do with religion. I had already acquired a religious philosophy after studying anthropology, mythology, Saint Thomas Aquinas, other philosophers. My philosophy went something like this. When a child in Western culture is about six years old, if he is astute, it occurs to him at Christmas time that Santa Claus is a myth. No way could he get around the world in one night with a 7-reindeer-powered machine. Likewise, when astute Christians reach adulthood, they see Christianity as a myth. No matter how valid the tenets of the faith are, it is a myth. No way could Noah's Ark have contained the mountain goats and lamas respectively from

Sgt. Nelson McAvoy

the Himalayas in India and the Andes in South America. No way could the people of these regions have been put to any disadvantage because of their lack of exposure to Judo–Christian information. When I go to Hell I might meet this guy, "My name is Nelson, what's your name?"

"I'm Gudu; nice to meet you, Nelson."

"When did you get here, Gudu?"

"I been here for 231,816 years, 2 months and 13 days."

"How can you keep that straight?"

"That's easy to keep in my head, I'm good at math, but I'm not human. I got a bum rap. They had a review 1700 years ago. I had been in Purgatory before that, you know. My cell mate during the review was Saint Peter's grandmother. She told me she said, 'Peter, I took care of you when you were born and had I not, you wouldn't be here today. I was good to everybody all my life and now I have had to spend all these years in Purgatory and then Hell, just because I never heard of Christ, never got saved, you were not up here when I died. Why didn't you tell me about Jesus Christ so I could have been saved also?'" Gudu went on, "I keep telling them, I'm not human! My mother was *Homo erectus*. Now it's true that my dad was a Cro-Magnon but that only makes me half human. Besides, there are all these jurisdictional problems. I keep telling Saint Peter, the racial designation goes with the mother, not the father. There was also this guy, if you can call a non-human that, Homer was his name, in the cell with me and Saint Peter's grandmother. He was only 1/4th human and that was because this human came in and raped his great-grandmother. Not only that, but the family of the human who raped her said they did not think it was right for her to get an abortion. These *Homo erectus* had lots of good potions for abortion, you know. Homer said, "Look Saint Peter, The Humans insisted that my great-grandmother not get an abortion, even in case of rape and incest. He was a smooth talker and Saint Peter let him through. The last thing he said to me, he was crying, he said I really don't want to go to Heaven either. I am a pre-Human. There have been billions of us. Most of them are a much bigger part human than I am. I just want to be dead like any other animal. Why do the humans insist on us part humans going to Heaven or Hell? Why? Why did we have to stay in Purgatory until Christ came? Why? What's with these Christians? How could they be so self righteous? Worse than burning women at the stake by the thousands, they insist that a billion of us half humans have to go to Heaven or Hell."

The reason I did not want to kill people was because I didn't understand these things. If I shot someone, as he sat there and watched the blood run out, I knew he was not thinking about the platitudes either. So I chose not to go to OCS.

I was surprised by the cold Massachusetts nights in August. I had never been out of West Virginia except for basic training. Fort Devens was the training center for ASA. I could not sleep at nights because I spent all day every day at the Post Exchange (PX) drinking coffee, smoking cigarettes, and participating in discussions conducted by the round table of quasi-AWOL-recruits. In atmosphere, it was a cross between a college student center and an Army PX. We had finished our batteries of tests and were waiting in a repo-depot (replacement depot) for assignments to schools or otherwise. In the Army they have to keep you busy and organized all the time. That meant work details for the repo-depot. Mostly walking around with idiot sticks policing (cleaning up). In the morning after chow you fell in for announcements and details assignment. That meant after chow I split and walked to the PX. A group of quasi-AWOL likeminded from the repo-depot had a session there all day long. Very lively conversations.

The quasi-AWOL-repo-depot-recruits at the PX round table were sure we could work out definite answers to the problems of the World. At the round table most every day were John Katz, a recent graduate of Harvard Business School and his buddy Sean Degnan from New York City. Two other regulars who became good friends were Bob Powell and Moon Cha, both UCLA graduates. Bob was a physics major and Moon Cha was a linguist who had done his thesis on the Chang Dynasty. Bob was 6 feet, 2 inches and Moon Cha came up to his belt. In addition there would be 3 or 4 out of a couple dozen that showed up each day. There seemed to be clusters from Yale, Brown and Stanford Universities. About half were 2-year draftees and half 3-year enlistees with a US or an RA respectively in front of the serial number. It turned out that RA (regular army) instead of US in front of your serial number made a difference when you were getting shuffled around as a piece of paper. "Private, what's your serial number?" "RA13431799, sir." That was mine.

Gudu, Homer, and Saint Peter's Grandmother were attacked mercilessly by some for their sacrilegious attitudes. Another popular subject was the Brown vs. Board of Education trial that was going on. I thought, boy, we are going to get the answer to all the world's problems and especially the race problem in the USA. That was until one of the electrical engineers from Old Miss. referred to Bill McKinney's wife as a negress. "Negress, negress," Bill kept repeating. "You son of a bitch, you don't refer to John's sister as a Jewess. Moon Cha, is your wife a Chinkess"? By that time Bill's voice was up 20 decibels and all the customers in the PX lounge were entertained. Probably the NCO in charge of the PX called the 1st Sergeant at the repo-depot. I really had the feeling that the cadre didn't care what the recruits did as long as there was an image of everybody doing structured things on Post. After the details marched back and were dismissed it was safe to come back to the company area because there was lots of random walking around. We would come back from the PX, then go to chow, then fall in for evening formation. One of the announcements at the evening formation on the same day that Bill McKinney's negress was discussed was, "Private McAvoy, Private McKinney, . . . report at 0900 tomorrow to the First Sergeant. Another was, "We are required to announce (as if to say, but don't pay any attention to it) that the Inspector General will be available in the morning for interviews." Nine o'clock I was in the orderly room.

"What are you here for, Private?"

"To see the IG."

"What's your complaint?"

"Nothing Sergeant, I just want to let him know that I can do more for ASA as a research physicist than if they assign me as a radio operator." Just then the IG, a Major, walked out to the CO's office and started out the door.

"Major Johnson, sir," the sergeant said and the major stopped dead in his tracks with the door half open.

"Yes, sergeant,"

"There is a solder here who wishes an appointment."

The Major looked at me for a few seconds and reversed his steps and walked into a side office.

"In here, soldier," he said as he seated himself behind the plain small beat-up desk and threw his briefcase on it.

I came in and saluted and said, "Request permission to speak to the IG, sir."

"Be seated."

"Sir, when I took the battery of tests I know I did well on the radio operators test because, as an amateur radio operator, I receive 20 words a minute."

"I have a station too; what's your call sign?" said the Major.

"W8UOE," I lied; that was my teacher's call sign. I would have had to go to Washington, DC, to take the test and waste money so I just used anyone's call sign or made one up. The threat of Federal Agents coming up to West Virginia for any-thing other than hunting moonshine stills was never even considered. "You're from West Virginia, then?"

"Yes sir." (The 8 in the call sign was for WV). "If ASA has use for someone who can do advanced microwave antenna design, I might serve my country better."

"I see. Write that information along with your name, rank, and serial number on this form and leave it with the Sergeant."

"Yes sir."

"Dismissed," he said as he was writing without looking up. I saluted and left. No one was in the Company area and all the details were out so I headed for the PX. The next morning I was up at 06:00 hour, couldn't sleep. Good smells were com-ing from the mess hall. I went in the back way to the kitchen. Over at the big pots and pans sink, I started helping the KP (kitchen police) with pots and pans. For my meals at Fair-mont College, I did the pots and pans in the kitchen. Throw-ing a towel over my shoulder so the Mess Sergeant knew I was on KP duty, I went over and got a coffee and doughnut. I stayed on KP until the afternoon pots and pans and big alu-minum vats were clean. The Mess Sergeant had a Hillbilly accent so I fell in with him talking about hunting and fish-ing and trapping and worked thereafter from 0:600 to 14:00 hours each day and then went to the PX. That gave me a half day with the quasi-AWOL repo-depot roundtable discussion group and freed me from the anxiety of being AWOL. There was no way they could court martial me for being AWOL if I was on KP, whether I was assigned there or not. Worse case, I could have the Mess Sergeant speak for me.

In a few days I got orders to report to Hq. & Hq. Company, Arlington Hall Station, Arlington, VA. It was exhilarating just to be out on my own, even if it was just for a couple of days to find my own way to Washington, DC. I hitchhiked and kept my travel money. As a soldier with a duffle bag in those days, a hitchhiker never had to stand on the road more than a few minutes and it was exciting meeting all kinds of people. One of the most exhilarating things about being outside of West Virginia was the diversity of those you met and the excitement of learning about new people and their customs. It was the same excitement as reaching out over the world with a "ham" radio. In Washington I found no local bus drivers who knew where Arlington Hall Station was.

Arlington Hall Station, Arlington Virginia, World War II Code Breakers

It would never have occurred to me to get a taxi. I did not know that others were not so frugal and stingy as the Scots. The bus driver that took me across the Potomac River to Roslyn, VA, said, "You'll have to get a taxi." I did and the taxi let me off in the pitch dark that I later found out was the intersection of Glebe Road and Route 50 (Arlington Blvd.). There was a small light in the distance and I walked toward it. It was a guard house. I showed my orders, drew bed clothes from the duty NCO, and slept soundly. These days, when I drive across the intersection of Glebe Road and Arlington Boulevard, tears come to my eyes, but it is hardly recognizable, having become a busy metropolitan neighborhood.

Hq. & Hq. Company was composed of the cooks, motor pool, base maintenance, MPs (military police) and ASA operative enlisted men. ASA operatives and cooks lived in one barracks and the MPs in another. There were more MPs than any other personnel because everyone who was on the base who was not a permanent staff had to be escorted at all times by an MP. The permanent buildings of Arlington Hall were an old and beautiful girl's prep school that had been requisitioned during World War II and was the place where code breaking during World War II was centered.

I had a second set of orders the second day and was escorted to the offices of a civilian, Neil Ganzert. Neil was a Virginia Military Institute graduate and was an Army major (or maybe a Colonel) in radio intelligence during World War II. He was the only person remotely close to a father figure that I ever had. My first week at work he wrote orders to give me the MOS (military occupational specialty) of a Traffic Analyst.

Settling into the bachelor life of a young adult in Washington DC was the culture shock of a lifetime. Before the shock had subsided, in a few weeks I got orders to report to the Army Language School in Monterey, California. So that was where I would have been sent had I not gone to the IG. In ASA, the administrative and operational aspects of the organization were kept completely separate on the basis of one's "need to know." Instead of going to Neil Ganzert and showing him my orders, I just left. This time instead of hitchhiking I found out that I could travel from Bolling Air Force Base on a MATS (military air transport system) flight. I found that out from a Connecticut Avenue singles bar, where the Bolling Field personnel hung out. On the grounds of Monterey I kicked my first soccer ball. By the barracks where the German language students resided there was a soccer game in progress. The ball came at me and I reached down and scooped it up. A player came over and said, "Don't do that."

"Don't do what?"

"Don't pick a ball up when it is rolled to you," he said. I looked at him with a smirk and said, "Don't roll it to me if you don't want me to pick it up?"

"I see you're so slow witted you'll flunk out in no time."

I didn't want to flunk out in the worst way; the whole place was sunshine, palm trees, beaches, and gorgeous girls. Talk about culture shock, the easy ways of California absolutely blew my mind. I would walk along the beach at night and stop at each little group of young people dancing to a portable radio. Of course no uniforms off post. I saw Moon Cha from the quasi-AWOL-repo-depot Fort Devens gang. "Moon Cha, what you doing out here," we walked along together, two of his steps to one of mine.

"I'm assigned here."

"What you teaching."

"I can't tell you."

"Moon Cha, what the hell you mean, you can't tell me?" I laughed.

"You don't have any need to know," he said seriously.

"Moon Cha, you're carrying that 'need to know' thing a little too far aren't you? When I said, what are you teaching, you didn't say 'I'm not teaching.' Here we are at the Army

Language School, you have a degree in Chinese Literature, you once said you speak 22 dialects."

"I teach," he finally said, and I knew not to ask any more questions. In ASA they took the "need to know" seriously. It caused mix ups sometimes. The Company Commander at Arlington Hall had no idea what the soldiers under him did during the day. That is probably why I was assigned to the Commanding General of ASA, General Reicheldorfer under Neil Ganzert with an MOS of Traffic Analyst, arranged by the IG in the repo-depot in Fort Devens and my original assignment from the repo-depot in Fort Devens was to the Army Language School in Monterey, CA. One did not get canceled probably as a result of this "need to know" rule. As you will see, that was soon corrected in no uncertain terms.

Back to Moon Cha. I followed him around in the evenings because Chinese food was so wonderful and such a novelty for me. I remember in school one time the teacher asked a girl what the four main food groups were, she said, beans, tomatoes, corn and potatoes. Chinese food was more than beans, tomatoes, corn, and potatoes. Dinner was a social thing and free at all the Chinese restaurants when I was with Moon Cha. The help huddled around Moon Cha and he did not order from the menu.

"What do you tell those people to get them all to huddle around the table and give you free food, Moon Cha?"

"In China family is name, and name is everything. I just speak their dialect and tell them my name is so-and-so and my grandfather was someone who had the same name as their grandfather and lived in the same village. That makes me family and I can have what I want, least of all food. Most of the restaurants in an area are run by related families."

One afternoon I was called out of class to report to the Company Commander. "Private McAvoy reporting as ordered, sir," as I saluted.

"You're not a private anymore, you are a sergeant, and congratulations."

"Yes sir."

"And I also have orders for you to report forthwith back to Headquarters and Headquarters Company at Arlington Hall Station. That's all pri . . , I mean, Sergeant."

"But, Sir, I am stationed here and want to graduate with m . . ."

"Dismissed," he cut me off with a smirk. "I don't like it either, when they pull students out and stick them in a class in the middle of a program. Dismissed."

"Yes sir." I saluted did an about face and went out devastated. As I went out of the Orderly Room the Sgt. Major said, "Here's your orders," as he slid them across the desk.

"Why would they want to make a snot nosed kid like you a sergeant? I was in the Army seven years before I made sergeant." I was so upset about having to leave, I vented it on him. I stared at him for a pause and said, "It's because I like killing people faster and better than you, Serg." I did not go back to class, took my last long walk on the beach with tears running down my face. When I came back, "Moon Cha, let's not eat chow, let's go get some Chinese food."

"I can't, I gotta study." He knew something was wrong. "What's up?"

"What do you mean, you got to study. You're the teacher."

"I'm not a teacher yet. I'm going in front of a board first to see if I am good enough to teach." My feelings were hurt that he was not going to spend my last evening with me and the Chinese restaurant, and walk the beach.

"I thought you were not going to tell me anything because I had no 'need to know'?" He just stared quizzically.

"Well, I don't like it here too much. I'm going back to Arlington Hall. And on my way out I'll stop by the restaurant and tell them your name is Moon Cha and you been lying just to get free meals." Then I walked out, checked out of the post, packed my duffle bag, went to the Greyhound Station and got a ticket to an Air Force Base for a MATS flight.

It was September 1st. I had to report on/or about the fourth. I was home in two days. The next morning, it was crisp, I was on the porch looking down the Tygart River at a flock of geese just above the water. For a speed of 15 miles an hour, about 20 feet per second, I was wondering if each was just in front of the bow wave of the one in front. I was trying to remember the slip stream pressure formula and that would tell me how much they would be pushed along by it, and consequently, how much energy used by the bird in front of them was reused by them. The mental calculations were constantly interrupted by pictures of girls in a bow wave, a surf. I kept having pictures of girls in the surf being pushed along by a wave, just as the geese did. Then I heard Uncle Joe.

"Hi, Uncle Joe."

"What are you doing here? You just joined the Army. Every time I turn around, you're home again. You just came home for your Grandpa's funeral and now you're home again. Did you go AWOL?" I ignored that.

"Do you know why the geese fly in a V instead of one behind the other?

"It's easier going, or they wouldn't do it."

"Why," I queried.

"I don't know why, I'm no goose. Your whole life you been going around asking why, every time someone says something."

"Well, I know why on this one; I just wanted to know if others commonly knew it. It's because they are in the slip stream of the one in front and the slip stream pushes them along just like the surf pushes a surfer along. That saves them a lot of gas."

"Well, if that's so then why didn't the pilots fly to their target in a geese formation to save gas? God knows they need-ed to save gas," Uncle Joe asked.

"It's because the pilot can't stay in the right place of the slip stream. The surfer, she has to constantly be adjusting and a goose can do that too."

With a big grin Uncle Joe said, "Why you been saying 'she', you been out surfing with some shes?"

"For the same reason you been saying goose instead of gander," I said as I started singing,

> Rooster's crowing on Sourwood Mountain,
> Hi de um de doodle o day.
> So many pretty girls, you can't count them,
> All the remi necon dinecen day.
> Old Gray Goose went down the river,
> Hi de um de doodle o day.
> If I'd a been a gander, I'd a gone with her,
> All the remi necon dinecen day.
> Old man Newman can I have your daughter
> Hi de um de doodle o day.
> To bake my bread and fetch my water.
> All the remi necon dinecen day.
> No Sir young Sir you can't have her.
> Hi de um de doodle o day.
> She won't work and do what she oughter.
> All the remi necon dinecen day.

I couldn't tell him anything about Monterey; like Moon Cha said, he didn't have any "need to know".

Two days to get to Arlington, so I put on my uniform to hitchhike to Fairmont College. Then I took it off. Hitchhiking would be easier but I didn't want to parade around campus and stand out. And then I realized, I got money for the bus, I don't have to hitchhike. So I caught the afternoon bus and spent the night there. I went down to the women's dorm, Marrow Hall, where I washed pots and pans as a student. At the repo-depot at Fort Devens, pots and pans got me out of details; at Marrow Hall, it got me in with the girls. In the basement of Marrow Hall there was the dining room, kitchen, some caretaker's rooms, and a large room right by the kitchen full of stored furniture. I washed pots and pans in the kitchen at Marrow Hall for free meals, but that's another story. I had not seen my girlfriend, Barbara Lobis (soon to be my wife), for two months.

Arlington Hall Station

I was right back in the same bunk at Arlington Hall. First thing I did was to sew on one set of sergeant stripes. Next weekend I could hitchhike to Grafton and let my Mum sew the rest on (I should write "sew on the rest"—no preposition at the end of the sentence. My English teacher in college told me that when editors tried to de-Anglo-Saxonize Winston Churchill's prepositions at the end of a sentence, he said, "That is the kind of nonsense up with which I will not put.") The next thing I did was to report to Neil Ganzert, my civilian boss. At the gate of the big old brick building where General Reicheldorfer and his staff were, the MP said, "Your badge isn't for this building, Sergeant?" It felt good, someone calling me sergeant.

"I just checked in last night, I have to pick up my permanent badge today. I want to see Mr. Ganzert on the General's Staff."

"Not without a badge." He picked up the phone, glanced in the phone book and dialed. "There is a Sergeant McAvoy at the gate to see you, sir . . . I can't, he has no badge. . . Mr. Ganzert will be right out," he said to me. I started pacing. Each pace was farther away as I concentrated on what had gone on there before I left.

"Where are you going, Sergeant?" the MP asked.

"Nowhere, just pacing."

"Well, please don't pace too far. Regulations say that if you call someone out of Headquarters, you cannot leave until they get here."

"OK, OK."

"Hi, Neil."

"Hi," we shake hands.

"I see you're a sergeant now. How did that happen?" He had a sparkle in his eye and I knew he had something to do with it.

"I hear you been all over the country. Out on the beach? Did you like the palm trees?"

"Loved them, and the girls, and the beach, and the whole scene."

"Let's take a little walk," as he headed out.

"Why didn't you tell me you had orders?" he asked.

"Well, there is the 'need to know' thing so I didn't know whether I was supposed to or not. Besides, I thought the General's staff got all the info," I lied.

"Your RTOP [research and technology operating plan] went through."

What he was talking about was the work I did during the time I was first at Arlington Hall. Neil Ganzert had the RDF (radio direction finding) part of traffic analysis. In other words, suppose there was a transmitter in Ireland and there were three listening stations receiving the signal. One in Belgium, one in England, and one in Norway. Suppose the average reading of all the direction finders pointed to Dublin. How big of a circle would you draw around Dublin that would give the General Staff a 50–50 chance that the transmitter was within the circle? Or how big would a circle be for a 90% likelihood that the target was within that circle? Neil Ganzert and I proposed a plan to take DF bearings samples from our cooperative transmitters and make a study to recommend a way to be quantitative. We had submitted as an RTOP and it was approved. I had left after the RTOP was submitted and left Neil Ganzert with no one to do the study. So he started trying to get people, including finding where I had gone, and got me back. And that was the work I did for the next year. An enlisted man was particularly suited for the job, as it turned out, because he could go among the radio operators and watch what they did without an officer or civilian hanging over his shoulder. In fact, one of the staff officers suggested that I also make a list of any of the DF operators who did not do his job well. I must have had a strange look on my face because he said, "What's wrong with that, Sergeant? Getting you back here was a mess. First we had to find you. The Adjacent's office got your assignment from the Fort Devens Testing Officer. Then the Adjacent wanted to know why I wanted you, a recent recruit. I had to explain that you helped write the RTOP and were needed to carry out the study."

"That's what I have to do? I have to give up California beaches, surfing, Chinese food, soccer, and language school just so ASA can have unified DF procedures?" I pouted despondently.

"No, you could go to Korea as a dogface." I said no more and we walked over to a diner on Glebe and Arlington Boulevard, our routine for the next year to come.

I settled into the barracks. In the barracks at Arlington Hall Station, the cryptographers, linguists, and experts of the enlisted ranks, about half draftees and three year regular army, lived in the upstairs of the barracks. They had arranged wall units in ways that make private rooms while the cooks and motor pool personnel lived downstairs with rows of bunks. I think the more resourceful soldiers upstairs went to the woodworking hobby shop on post and made the partitions with wardrobes and chest of draws. The barracks houses all had the same pattern. There was a cast system. There was a large MP contingency because everyone other than permanent employees had an MP escort at all time. They had their own quarters. Another unique thing was that the upstairs soldiers, a tight knit bunch went together and rented a large suite just off post on Columbia Pike. It was walking distance. It was not so much for their use but usually there would be some friends coming into Washington DC as tourists. It was a great place for parties. And surprisingly, it was kept clean and tidy and well stocked. With two dozen soldiers or more, it was only $10 a month or so. But cost had nothing to do with it. Most of the operatives, the upstairs gang, were well-to-do. A few stayed there all the time but most thought our upstairs barracks arrangement was gemütlichkeit.

We will come back to this situation later. Upstairs were young men of very diverse backgrounds. Remember, except for basic training I had never been out of West Virginia. Had never taken SAT tests or the likes. I had never been around any college graduates except my school mates and professors. Many of the upstairs gang were world travelers, well-to-do, sophisticated people who spoke many languages. We made our social life by entertaining in our Columbia Pike suite and our preferred hangouts on Connecticut Ave. in Washington. Cars were always available. One weekend I went home and the state policeman wrote me out a driver's license without a test. But I always hitchhiked, loved to hitchhike.

In the barracks we shared the bathrooms and showers with the cooks. Many were amazed and curious about the cooks. That was their first time to have the opportunity to be around working class people. All young people were included in the draft. They must have sent only those that tested low to the cook's school. I am ashamed now that I used to manipulate the cooks to get them to talk about the kikes, niggers, wops, hunkies, dagos, spicks, and polocks. For example, when I was alone with the cooks I would rant and rave and teach them that Franklin Roosevelt was the culprit that gave women suffrage. Then, when the upstairs gang was around, I would get them to tell how F.D.R. was the perpetrator of women winning suffrage. It looked like innocent fun then and I saw the hate mongers and racists among them as innocuous. Little could I have imagined that in 40 years, many of the quasi-AWOL-repo-depo and "upstairs gang" would become part of the business and conservative political movement that would hook up with those from the "downstairs gang" who were the hate mongers and racists, and champion the "Reagan Revolution."

I put my issued kit in the foot locker and locked it, to be opened only if there was an inspection, all except two wool uniforms (Ike jacket types) that I kept on hangers. From the PX, I bought 12 white dress shirts; five khaki pants; 5 khaki short pants; two two-piece sets of wool long underwear; five pairs of heavy wool socks; cotton underwear and light socks and a Sheaffer white-dot-Balance, 14 K gold fine point nib fountain pen, and a 6 inch long "toad sticker" pocket knife that weighed 5 ounces (the weight of a baseball, I could stick it into the side of a hay bale at baseball pitching distances). From a clothing store I bought a light weight navy blue blazer;

one light and one heavy wool sweater; a heavy Harris Tweed wool sports coat; a pair of brown loafers; a pair of white tennis shoes; a few white handkerchiefs; a brown fedora hat; and five white cotton (two inch brim all around) tennis hats.

The only other worldly possession I had was a Hamilton gold pocket watch that my parents had bought me for high school graduation. They bought me a pocket watch because my father anticipated me being a farmer. He always said that I would be his retirement investment. He would buy me a mule and 40 acres and he could sit on the front porch when he was old. Farmers and railroaders wore pocket watches; everybody else had since turned to wrist watches. The other five siblings got wrist watches. I gave it to my grandson, Kyle Patrick McAvoy, for his high school graduation in 2003. If he wants, I'll get him a mule and 40 acres and he can live off the fat of the land.

No other worldly possessions did I want or need. Khaki short or long pants and a white shirt with the sleeves rolled up were perfect summer clothes for casual or sportswear. For cooler weather I had a light wool sweater. I also had a nice wool army issued sweater. Colder weather, I had two sets of long-johns and a heavy sweater and tweed jacket if need be. For more formal wear, I had white shirts, tie and blazer or tweed jacket. For even more formal wear, a uniform is always appropriate; a tux could always be rented. My wardrobe was designed around the Fort Meyer Quartermaster laundry service. Fort Meyer is adjacent to Arlington Hall Station and houses the troops that do the formal procedures in Washington and Arlington Cemetery. All of my khakis, white shirts and small clothes were put into the quartermaster laundry free or at minimal cost every week. I just left them in Headquarters Company Orderly Room on Monday and they came back on Wednesday. Khakis and white shirts came out as stiff

as cardboard and really looked good. The look, the manner-
isms, and the speech I affected were Ivy League. No one had
an inkling that I was a West Virginia hillbilly, no one except
a few astute individuals who watched me manipulating the
downstairs bunch. No one knew I was a kindred part of the
downstairs crowd—the cooks and the motorpool hillbillies.

I ate free in the mess hall and ink for my pen was at the
post office, the orderly room, or at my desk at work. Never before or since have had I had such a worry-free logistic arrangement to take care of my personal needs. One might think this
preoccupation implies obsession with an organized life. Just
the opposite is true. If they had invented Attention Deficit
Disorder, I would have been the original member of the disorder. I leave things around and forget where I put things. I had
to be a world traveler on this job. I was off to London, off to
Berlin, off to Korea, off to Fort Devens, off to Naval Security
Service on Nebraska Avenue next to American University,
off to Vint Hill Farms, a listening post for navel transmitters,
near Warrenton VA where my sister lived and taught school.
I unconsciously combated my absentmindedness. I did not at
the time know I was absentminded or had ADD. But I could
keep things straight if I had to. I learned, I realize now, little
tricks. I do not consider this as a shortcoming or a disorder.
My mind is not always cluttered with details; that is not a
shortcoming. Because of my ADD, I have been distracted,
where was I? My pen, my watch, my orders, and a simple kit
of civilian and military clothes minimized discombobulat-
ing. Fifty years hence, and I still wake up from a dream in a
cold sweat. I dream that I am eating breakfast in a diner at
the counter with a locked briefcase clutched between my
feet. The next thing I know, in my dream, is that I am walking
down the street and forgot the briefcase! It was an exciting
life, full of culture shock. A 22-year-old man who never met

a stranger and who had ridden in a car only two times in his life was now traveling all over the world by himself and had Ivy Leaguers as bosom buddies. Fridays I would usually work on my RDF (antenna) studies at Vint Hill Farm. My brother-in-law, Brady Corrothers, was a member of the Old Dominion Hunt. An Army uniform was proper attire for fox hunting and someone always had a horse that needed exercising. (Gen. George Patton was once Master of the Hunt.) Also, in the bitter cold of winter Vint Hill Farm had a large swimming pool and a few hundred WACs (or maybe WAVES) stationed there. For some reason the mess at Vint Hill Farm and the NCO Mess in the French Sector of Berlin had the best food in the world. Besides Vint Hill Farm, my other two favorite places to go were Christchurch, England, Signals Research Lab, and Fort Devens, MA. The former to play football in the park and the later to have a hitchhiking experience. What a wonderful life for a young man, football (soccer), fox hunting, meeting new people of all kinds, and of course Washington DC was full of young girls that have since been replaced by computers. Connecticut Avenue had rows of apartment buildings, about three girls to an apartment. Computers have not been a complete replacement.

I had already been told that a new agency, National Security Agency, was going to take over the combined work of the Army Security Agency, located at Arlington Hall Station; the Naval Security Service, whose headquarters was at Dupont Circle where Homeland Security is now housed; and the Air Force Security Service at Bolling Field. I knew this, of course, because my sole job was to work out a procedures manual for radio direction finding for land, sea and airplane receivers and their relative accuracies.

Because of the intelligence fiasco re the Chinese invasion of November 1950, one of the tasks was to work out procedures to be more quantitative. That, we thought at first could be done by calculating the radiation pattern of the Crossed-U-Adcock antenna used and working out an angle spread in which the transmitter was likely to be. In other words, a graph of 10, 20, 30, 60 degrees versus probability or likelihood that the transmitter was within that spread. Two receivers 90 degrees apart would give you an interception area versus probability. I pointed out that in addition a field study would have to be made because our received bearings from known targets did not agree with the theoretical predictions. In some cases they were better and some cases they were worse. There were too many variables for Neil Ganzert to stick his neck out and just give the ideal theoretical results. Signal strength, multiple ionospheric conditions, operator ability, reflections, and many other things required field studies. This was especially true if bearings were to be from ships, planes, and on the ground. It was my job to put all this together.

Chapter 3. NSA 1953–1997

There was one staff meeting in the spring of 1953 that sticks out in my memory and has haunted me ever since. Sometimes I would go along with Neil Ganzert to meetings where questions about our improvements in direction finding assessments might have been asked; and how we were going to coordinate the DF of the three services with the NSA. This was during the time of negotiations for a peace settlement in Korea. The settlement was final on July 27, 1953. From the early months of 1953 through June, the evenings were exciting, hanging out with the girls that lived on Connecticut Avenue. Sometimes I would not get in until the wee hours of the morning but by eight o'clock results were in from the analysis of the previous days traffic of General One Hung Lo's (the name some traffic analysis had assigned him) 46th Army of the Peoples Republic of China (PRC). The staff meeting in question was before July 15, I remember because we had built up a picture, this time with probability numbers. Sure enough, General Van Fleet's 8th Army used this information to reinforce areas of PRC attack on July 15 and we clobbered them. Some say this catalyzed the signing on July 27.

So Neil took me along to this staff meeting because he thought there might be details they wanted to know about One Hung Lo's PRC deployment. It was not about that at all. The meeting was about introducing the signal intelligence community to the newly formed NSA. This is one of the most memorable days of my life. I go over it and over it. General Harry Reicheldorfer the Arlington Hall Commandant and ASA Commander introduced guests from the Joint Chiefs and the White House. He then said, in effect (I cannot quote him directly),

> Gentlemen, there has been a lot of talk and misinformation about the newly formed National Security Agency, that was set up by President Truman just before he left office. Many of you will be involved with, and indeed become part of, this new agency. We have set up plans for peacetime collection, analysis, and distribution of intelligence. It includes the services organizations, Army Security Agency, Air Force Security Service and the Navy Security Service. This structure is an adaptation to the new peacetime situation we find ourselves in as well as the possible looming USSR menace. The NSA will be headed by a three star general under the Department of Defense and will also be a member of the National Security Council which advises the Department of State and all other relevant Executive Branch needs.
>
> Under the Eisenhower administration we have begun to solidify plans for the detailed operation of the NSA and CIA and other intelligence organizations. This conflict with Korea and now China has taught us the bitter lesson of isolating COMINT (communication intelligence) from other aspects of intelligence. At the beginning of the conflict we had little if any linguistic or cultural grounding, operations people, or behind-the-line

informants. We shall never let that happen again. We have learned that we cannot separate COMINT from other information sources such as ideological informants, paid informants, local monitoring, and the likes. The NSA will have a permanent cadre of operations for all possible future belligerents. President Truman's Executive Order setting up the NSA did not delineate details. Under President Eisenhower we have to come up with a detailed plan for what the NSA will not do and what to leave to the Central Intelligence Agency. As you know, the CIA was established a few years ago by Congress as a civilian agency mostly recruited from the Office of Strategic Service that was abolished after the War. CIA will continue OSS type of operations. They, like OSS are not informational orientated, they are aggressive operations oriented. Intelligence, in the sense of acquiring information on which reasonable decisions can be made, will be the purview of the NSA. [I can remember this quote:] "In other words gentlemen, CIA is not an intelligence agency, the NSA will be this country's intelligence agency. I repeat, this conflict in Korea and our hostility with the USSR has taught us that we no longer productively separate COMINT and HUMINT." All belligerents of the Second World War have learned to be more sophisticated with encrypting and transmitting messages. Another consequence of the War is that there are now sympathizers located in all nations willing to risk everything for us and we must learn to make the most of it.

In the questions and answers session it kept being emphasized that the name Central Intelligence Agency was chosen to misdirect. It was pointed out that CIA was set up by an act of Congress and, therefore, Congress had oversight. The NSA was set up by Executive Order, was commanded by a three star general (they all wanted to know about this) and had a (classified) budget inside DoD, although they are a separate agency and not under DoD auspices. There is no Congressional oversight of the NSA.

It will be very difficult, probably impossible, for me to explain why this lack of Congressional oversight, indeed even deception of Congress and everyone outside the "intelligence community," was assumed to be imperative. It was generally agreed that it was imperative to violate the United States Constitution by deceiving and intentionally misleading Congress about the spending of enormous amounts of federal treasure and illegal activities. First off, a nation cannot build up an intelligence apparatus directed at an adversary in the same manner as one does the armed forces. The recent Korean War history just screamed this fact out at us.

As a short review of the Korean War, when it became clear in mid-August 1945 that Japan intended to surrender, U.S. policy makers began to make arrangements for peripheral areas occupied by Japan. One of the thorniest problems was the status of Korea. The peninsula had been an independent nation for centuries before the Japanese took it as a colony in 1910. In August 1945, Soviet forces were fighting the Japanese military on the China-Korea border, and it appeared that the Red Army might occupy all of Korea. The U.S. solution was a temporary division of the country. Americans would take the Japanese surrender in the southern sector, Soviet troops in the north. After a suitable—but undefined—period in which Koreans would be prepared for self-rule, both armies would withdraw. The Soviets agreed to this plan, and Korea was divided on either side of the 38th parallel. However, as the Cold War developed, the peninsula became a pawn in a larger, international ideological struggle. After three years, the United States turned the problem over to the United Nations, which mandated elections to decide on a unified government in Korea. UN-sponsored elections led to the formation of the Republic of Korea (ROK) on August 15, 1948, under President Syngman Rhee, with its capital in Seoul. North Korea declined to participate in the UN elections and formed its own government, the Democratic People's Republic of Korea (DPRK), with Kim Il-sung as its leader and its capital in Pyongyang. The next two years were marked by struggle on many levels—military, political, and ideological. Small unit clashes and armed incursions along the 38th parallel were frequent. Both the ROK and the DPRK built military forces, but there was a difference: the USSR supplied armor and aircraft to Pyongyang, while the U.S. denied them to Seoul.

The United States deliberately excluded South Korea from the defensive perimeter it was drawing around the Pacific Ocean area. The ROK, said U.S. officials, should depend on the United Nations for support.

Finally, in the early hours of June 25, 1950, the Korean People's Army (KPA) crossed the dividing line in strength and began pushing southward toward Seoul. After some initial resistance, the ROK Army gave way before the larger, stronger KPA, and retreat became a rout. President Harry S. Truman and his advisers assumed the USSR had directed the attack and that this was the opening move in a wider war. At that point, the U.S. reversed its policy and intervened militarily to support the ROK. The U.S. persuaded the United Nations to call for assistance in repelling North Korea's aggression, and a number of other UN members sent troops or supporting forces. After a period of retreat, General Walton Walker, in command of the U.S. Eighth Army, stabilized the lines around a defensible area that came to be known as the "Pusan Perimeter." Deployed largely along the meandering Naktong River, Walker moved his forces quickly and astutely to blunt repeated North Korean attacks.

On 15 September 1950, a USMC/Army amphibious force, spearheaded by Marines, striking according to General Douglas MacArthur's plans, conducted one of the greatest feats of American arms ever, an amphibious landing behind North Korean lines at the port of Inchon. This operation, combined with a breakout from the Pusan Perimeter, smashed the DPRK's military forces. UN forces, primarily American and South Korean troops, crossed into North Korean territory in pursuit of their retreating enemy, despite warnings from Communist China to remain below the 38th parallel. In November, as U.S. and South Korean forces approached the China–Korea border, the People's Liberation Army (PLA) struck them in force, sending the UN army in a precipitous retreat southward. In the spring of 1951, UN forces reestablished a stable line of resistance with the communist armies at roughly the midpoint of the Korean peninsula. Both sides entrenched. The Korean War continued for more than two years, but consisted largely of limited offensive operations, characterized by only small gains and losses, to capture or defend particular points of real estate.

The war ended in August 1953, after more than three years of combat, with the signing of a truce agreement and the exchange of prisoners. During the war and in postwar investigations, there were many charges that U.S. intelligence had failed in the Korean War, not once, but twice. Critics charged that American intelligence organizations had failed to give warnings of the initial North Korean attack in June 1950 and failed again when the Chinese entered the war in October 1950.

When we got involved, there were no Korean linguists, no maps, no Korean typewriters, no dictionaries and no way of knowing who in Korea were really trustworthy. We had just been burned by using a non-citizen in the Russian Section at

Arlington Hall Station. During the era of the Battle of Stalingrad in 1942, the Russians were so desperate for supplies that the pages of random numbers used for encryption were printed over and over again for code books. In our story about breaking JN-25 before the Battle of Midway, it was noted that the Japanese yeomen on board men-of-war used the same pages in their books of random numbers over and over. The Russians did the equivalent by reprinting old pages. So by 1948 we were breaking the Russian messages routinely. Then along comes William Weisband. He was born in Odessa, in 1908, of Russian Jewish parents. He immigrated to the United States in the 1920s and became a naturalized United States citizen in 1938. He joined the United States Army in 1942 and was assigned to signals intelligence duties. From 1941 to 1942, Weisband was the NKVD agent handler for Jones Orin York, who worked at the Northrop Corporation. After joining the U.S. Army's Signals Intelligence Service (SIS) in 1942, he performed signals intelligence and communications security duties in North Africa and Italy, where he made some important friends before returning to the "Russian Section" at Arlington Hall, where SIS had established its headquarters in June, 1942. Although not a cryptanalyst himself, as a "linguist adviser" who spoke fluent Russian, Weisband worked closely with cryptanalysts. The Soviets apparently had monitored Arlington Hall's Russian Section since at least 1945, when Weisband joined the unit. Weisband's earliest reports on the work being done by U.S. cryptanalysts on the Soviet diplomatic code were probably sketchy, but after Weisband began passing information on the work of the Russian Section, Soviet authorities changed their diplomatic code and decryptions dried up. Weisband's role as a Soviet agent was not discovered by counterintelligence officers until 1950.

It was clear to us after the Korean War what was needed. The process was started by a memorandum to the National Security Council, dated 10 December 1951, General Walter Bedell Smith, Director of Central Intelligence (DCI), recommending an overall review of United States intelligence activities. The proposal was forwarded to President Truman. Three days later, on 13 December 1951, Truman directed Secretary of State Dean G. Acheson and Secretary of Defense Robert A. Lovett, assisted by Smith, to review in depth the intelligence activities of the United States.

On 28 December 1951, in response to Truman's request, Acheson and Lovett established the Brownell Committee to study the existing structure and make recommendations. George A. Brownell, an eminent attorney in New York City, headed the committee. Brownell served as chairman, assisted by Charles E. (Chip) Bohlen, counselor, State Department; William H. Jackson, special assistant to the DCI; and Brigadier General John Magruder, USA (Ret), special assistant to the secretary of defense. The CIA and the Department of State provided the four staff members for the committee, all of whom had served previously in the special intelligence branches of the Army or Navy. The military organizations had no representation on the Brownell Committee or on its support staff, not even the Joint Chiefs of Staff. Logistically, during the period of the survey, the Brownell Committee and its support staff resided at CIA (a civilian organization) and received administrative support from the CIA. This was very telling of where President Truman was coming from.

Within six months, the Brownell Committee completed its report. It stressed the need for the unification of U.S. intelligence responsibilities and recommended a major overhaul of the existing structure. The final Brownell Report completely demolished the concept of unification as it existed under

Armed Forces Security Agency (AFSA) — the combined effort during the Korean War. During the next four months, extended negotiations took place among the representatives of CIA, DoD, Department of State, and the Director of AFSA over the exact wording of the implementing directives to be issued by the president. The Joint Chiefs of Staff were also excluded from these discussions. Ten months after the establishment of the Brownell Committee, Truman, accepting the report, issued two directives that led to the establishment of the National Security Agency. There would be a centralized authority for intelligence activities, and the civilian authorities would play a major role in directing the scope of the NSA's operations.

In conclusion, the directive clearly established the national rather than the solely military character of the NSA. It greatly expanded administrative and operational controls over all U.S. cryptology activities but did not restrict the extent of the NSA activities in other aspects of intelligence gathering such as infiltration and the planting of agents. For the first time, the director acquired the authority to issue instructions directly to military units without going through military command channels. From the outset, the designers of the NSA charter clearly recognized that complete unification would be impossible because of the dependence upon the military structures to man field stations. The Brownell Committee, as well as the drafters of the implementing presidential directive, supported the services' traditional position that they must control the close and direct intelligence support of the forces in the field.

Great pains were taken to obscure the NSA budget in the overall DoD budget by making it top secret and to restrict Congressional oversight by, for the first and only time in US history, establishing an agency by presidential edict.

In other words, at this meeting at Arlington Hall Station, where I was a lowly sergeant and a fly on the wall, it was explained that the NSA would:

- Be a permanent peace time civilian intelligence agency with permanent "sections" for the dress, language, customs, history, and culture of each possible advocacy.

- Infiltrate the institutions of these countries solely for non-disruptive information gathering.

- Foster personal ties with influential people in each of the countries.

- Maintain NSA employees in industrial and educational organizations in order to have a knowledge base and technically keep abreast. Especially computer expertise.

- Develop a unique and clandestine way to bring information back from all parts of the world (e.g. the NSA satellite system).

- Non-interventionist policy to facilitate clandestineness.

- A "cut-out" organization to insulate the source when information is provided to proper U.S. authorities (CIA).

CIA Operations

Today this seems outlandish to everyone, I know; and all that I knew who were involved in this planning are either dead or senile. You do not need to know what the original planning stages of the NSA were to see that these things are true. All you have to do is notice the history of these two agencies from 1952 to as least 2010. All one has to do is look at the highlights of publicized activities of these two agencies over this 58 years[10].

---

[10] *Killing Hope: U.S. Military and CIA Interventions since World War II*, Common Courage Press, 1995.

1947: CIA created

Congress passed the National Security Act of 1947, creating the Central Intelligence Agency and National Security Council. The CIA is accountable to the president through the NSC. Its charter allows the CIA to "perform such other functions and duties as the National Security Council may from time to time direct." This loophole opens the door to covert action and dirty tricks.

1947: Greece

President Truman requests military aid to Greece to support right-wing forces fighting communist rebels. For the rest of the Cold War, Washington and the CIA will back notorious Greek leaders with deplorable human rights records.

1948: Covert-action wing created

The CIA recreates a covert action wing, innocuously called the Office of Policy Coordination, led by Wall Street lawyer Frank Wisner. According to its secret charter, its responsibilities include: propaganda, economic warfare, direct action, including sabotage, anti-sabotage, demolition and evacuation procedures; subversion against hostile states, including assistance to underground resistance groups, and support of indigenous anti-communist elements in threatened countries of the free world.

1948: Italy

The CIA corrupts democratic elections in Italy, where Italian communists threaten to win the elections. The CIA buys votes, broadcasts propaganda, threatens and beats up opposition leaders, and infiltrates and disrupts their organizations. It works—the communists are defeated.

1949: Radio Free Europe

The CIA creates its first major propaganda outlet, Radio Free Europe. Over the next several decades, its broadcasts are

so blatantly false that for a time it is considered illegal to publish transcripts of them in the US.

1953: Iran

CIA overthrows the democratically elected Mohammed
Mossadegh in a military coup, after he threatened to nation-
alize British oil. The CIA replaces him with a dictator, the
Shah of Iran, whose secret police, SAVAK, is as brutal as the
Gestapo.

1953: Operation MK-ULTRA

Inspired by North Korea's brainwashing program, the
CIA begins experiments on mind control. The most notorious
part of this project involves giving LSD and other drugs to
American subjects without their knowledge or against their
will, causing several to commit suicide. However, the operation involves far more than this. Funded in part by the Rockefeller and Ford foundations, research includes propaganda,
brainwashing, public relations, advertising, hypnosis, and
other forms of suggestion.

1954: Guatemala

CIA overthrows the democratically elected Jacob Arbenz
in a military coup. Arbenz has threatened to nationalize the
Rockefeller-owned United Fruit Company, in which CIA Director Allen Dulles also owns stock. Arbenz is replaced with
a series of right-wing dictators whose bloodthirsty policies
will kill over 100,000 Guatemalans in the next 40 years.

1954–1958: North Vietnam

CIA officer Edward Lansdale spends four years trying to
overthrow the communist government of North Vietnam, using all the usual dirty tricks. The CIA also attempts to legiti-
mize a tyrannical puppet regime in South Vietnam, headed by
Ngo Dinh Diem. These efforts fail to win the hearts and minds
of the South Vietnamese because the Diem government is op-
posed to land reform and poverty reduction measures. The

CIA escalates American intervention until our gradual entry into a Vietnam War.

1956: Hungary

Radio Free Europe incites Hungary to revolt by broadcasting Khrushchev's Secret Speech, in which he denounced Stalin. It also hints that American aid will help the Hungarians fight. This aid fails to materialize as Hungarians launch a doomed armed revolt, which only invites a major Soviet invasion. The conflict kills 7,000 Soviets and 30,000 Hungarians.

1957–1973: Laos

The CIA carries out approximately one coup per year trying to nullify Laos' democratic elections. The problem is the Pathet Lao, a leftist group with enough popular support to be a member of any coalition government. In the late 50s, the CIA even creates an "Army Clandestine" of Asian mercenaries to attack the Pathet Lao. After the CIA's army suffers numerous defeats, the US starts bombing, dropping more bombs on Laos than all the US bombs dropped in World War II. A quarter of all Laotians will eventually become refugees, many living in caves.

1959: Haiti

The CIA helps "Papa Doc" Duvalier become dictator of Haiti. He creates his own private police force, the "Tonton Macoutes," who terrorize the population with machetes. They will kill over 100,000 during the Duvalier family reign.

1961: The Bay of Pigs

The CIA sends 1,500 Cuban exiles to invade Castro's Cuba. But "Operation Mongoose" fails, due to poor planning, security and backing. The planners had imagined that the invasion would spark a popular uprising against Castro—which never happens. A promised US air strike also never occurs. This is the CIA's first public setback, causing President Kennedy to fire CIA Director Allen Dulles.

1961: Congo (Zaire)

The CIA assassinates the democratically elected Patrice Lumumba. However, public support for Lumumba's politics runs so high that the CIA cannot clearly install his opponents in power. Four years of political turmoil follow.

1963: Dominican Republic

Trujillo's business interests have grown so large (about 60 percent of the economy) that they have begun competing with American business interests. The CIA overthrows the democratically elected Juan Bosch in a military coup. The CIA installs a repressive, right wing junta. The CIA assassinates Rafael Trujillo, a murderous dictator Washington has supported since 1930. A popular rebellion breaks out, promising to reinstall Juan Bosch as the country's elected leader. The revolution is crushed when U.S. Marines land to uphold the military regime by force. The CIA directs everything behind the scenes.

1963: Ecuador

The CIA-backed military forces the democratically elected President Jose Velasco to resign. Vice President Carlos Arosemana replaces him; the CIA fills the now vacant vice presidency with its own man. A CIA-backed military coup overthrows President Arosemana, whose independent (not socialist) policies have become unacceptable to Washington. A military junta assumes command, cancels the 1964 elections, and begins abusing human rights.

1964: Brazil

A CIA-backed military coup overthrows the democratically elected government of Joao Goulart. The junta that replaces it will, in the next two decades, become one of the most bloodthirsty in history. General Castelo Branco will create Latin America's first death squads, or bands of secret police that hunt down "communists" for torture, interrogation and murder. Often these "communists" are no more than Branco's political opponents. Later it is revealed that the CIA trains the death squads.

1965: Indonesia

The CIA overthrows the democratically elected Sukarno with a military coup. The CIA has been trying to eliminate Sukarno since 1957, using everything from attempted assassination to sexual intrigue, for nothing more than his declaring neutrality in the Cold War. His successor, General Suharto, will massacre between 500,000 and 1 million civilians accused of being "communist." The CIA supplies the names of countless suspects.

1966: The Ramparts Affair

The radical magazine Ramparts begins a series of unprecedented anti-CIA articles. Among their scoops: the CIA has paid Michigan State University $25 million dollars to hire "professors" to train South Vietnamese students in covert police methods. MIT and other universities have received similar payments. Ramparts also reveal that the National Students' Association is a CIA front. Students are sometimes recruited through blackmail and bribery, including draft deferments.

1967: Greece

With the CIA's backing, the king removes George Papandreous as prime minister. Papandreous has failed to vigorously support U.S. interests in Greece. A CIA-backed military coup overthrows the government two days before the elections. The favorite to win was George Papandreous, the liberal candidate. During the next six years, the "reign of the colonels" - backed by the CIA - will usher in the widespread use of torture and murder against political opponents.

1968: Operation Chaos

The CIA has been illegally spying on American citizens since 1959, but with Operation CHAOS, President Johnson dramatically boosts the effort. CIA agents go undercover as student radicals to spy on and disrupt campus organizations protesting the Vietnam War. They are searching for Russian instigators, which they never find. CHAOS will eventually spy on 7,000 individuals and 1,000 organizations.

1968: Bolivia

A CIA-organized military operation captures legendary guerilla Che Guevara. The CIA wants to keep him alive for interrogation, but the Bolivian government executes him to prevent worldwide calls for clemency.

1969: Uruguay

The notorious CIA torturer Dan Mitrione arrives in Uruguay, a country torn with political strife. Whereas right-wing forces previously used torture only as a last resort, Mitrione convinces them to use it as a routine, widespread practice. "The precise pain, in the precise place, in the precise amount, for the desired effect," is his motto. The torture techniques he teaches to the death squads rival those of the Nazis. He eventually becomes so feared that revolutionaries will kidnap and murder him a year later.

1970: Cambodia

The CIA overthrows Prince Sihanouk, who is highly popular among Cambodians for keeping them out of the Vietnam War. He is replaced by CIA puppet Lon Nol, who immediately throws Cambodian troops into battle. This unpopular move strengthens once minor opposition parties like the Khmer Rouge, which achieves power in 1975 and massacres millions of its own people.

1971: Bolivia

After half a decade of CIA-inspired political turmoil, a CIA-backed military coup overthrows the leftist President Juan Torres. In the next two years, dictator Hugo Banzer will have over 2,000 political opponents arrested without trial, then tortured, raped and executed.

1972: The Case-Zablocki Act

Congress passes an act requiring congressional review of executive agreements. In theory, this should make CIA operations more accountable. In fact, it is only marginally effective.

1972: Cambodia

Congress votes to cut off CIA funds for its secret war in Cambodia.

1972: Watergate Break-in

President Nixon sends in a team of burglars to wiretap Democratic offices at Watergate. The team members have extensive CIA histories, including James McCord, E. Howard Hunt and five of the Cuban burglars. They work for the Committee to Reelect the President (CREEP), which does dirty work like disrupting Democratic campaigns and laundering Nixon's illegal campaign contributions. CREEP's activities are funded and organized by another CIA front, the Mullen Company.

1973: Chile

The CIA overthrows and assassinates Salvador Allende, Latin America's first democratically elected socialist leader. The problems begin when Allende nationalizes American-owned firms in Chile. ITT offers the CIA one million dollars for a coup (reportedly refused). The CIA replaces Allende with General Augusto Pinochet, who will torture and murder thousands of his own countrymen in a crackdown on labor leaders and the political left.

1973: CIA begins internal investigations

William Colby, the Deputy Director for Operations, orders all CIA personnel to report any and all illegal activities they know about. This information is later reported to Congress.

1973: CIA Director Helms Fired

President Nixon fires CIA Director Richard Helms for failing to help cover up the Watergate scandal. Helms and Nixon have always disliked each other. The new CIA director is William Colby, who is relatively more open to CIA reform.

1974: CHAOS exposed

Pulitzer Prize-winning journalist Seymour Hersh publishes a story about Operation CHAOS, the domestic surveillance and infiltration of anti-war and civil rights groups in the U.S. The story sparks national outrage.

1974: Angleton fired

Congress holds hearings on the illegal domestic spying efforts of James Jesus Angleton, the CIA's chief of counterintelligence. His efforts included mail-opening campaigns and secret surveillance of war protesters. The hearings result in his dismissal from the CIA.

1974: The Hughes Ryan Act

Congress passes an amendment requiring the president to report non-intelligence CIA operations to the relevant congressional committees in a timely fashion.

1975: Australia

The CIA helps topple the democratically elected, left-leaning government of Prime Minister Edward Whitlam. The CIA does this by giving an ultimatum to its Governor-General, John Kerr. Kerr, a longtime CIA collaborator, exercises his constitutional right to dissolve the Whitlam government. The Governor-General is a largely ceremonial position appointed by the Queen; the Prime Minister is democratically elected. The use of this archaic and never-used law stuns the nation.

1975: Angola

Eager to demonstrate American military resolve after its defeat in Vietnam, Henry Kissinger launches a CIA-backed war in Angola. Contrary to Kissinger's assertions, Angola is a country of little strategic importance and not seriously threatened by communism. The CIA backs the brutal leader Jonas Savimbi. This polarizes Angolan politics and drives his opponents into the arms of Cuba and the Soviet Union for survival. Congress will cut off funds in 1976, but the CIA is able to run the war off the books until 1984, when funding is legalized again. This entirely pointless war kills over 300,000 Angolans.

1976: "Inside the Company"

Philip Agee publishes a diary of his life inside the CIA. Agee had worked in covert operations in Latin America during the 60s, and details the crimes in which he took part.

1977: Congress investigates CIA wrongdoing

Public outrage compels Congress to hold hearings on CIA crimes. Senator Frank Church heads the Senate investigation ("The Church Committee"), and Representative Otis Pike heads the House investigation. (Despite a 98 percent incumbency reelection rate, both Church and Pike are defeated in the next elections.) The investigations lead to a number of reforms intended to increase the CIA's accountability to Congress, including the creation of a standing Senate committee on intelligence. However, the reforms prove ineffective, as the Iran/Contra scandal will show. It turns out the CIA can control, deal with or sidestep Congress with ease.

1978: The Rockefeller Commission

In an attempt to reduce the damage done by the Church Committee, President Ford creates the "Rockefeller Commission" to whitewash CIA history and propose toothless reforms. The commission's namesake, Nelson Rockefeller, is himself a major CIA figure. Five of the commission's eight members are also members of the Council on Foreign Relations, a CIA-dominated organization.

1979: Iran

The Shah of Iran is a longtime CIA puppet. His brutality helped cause the rise of Muslim fundamentalists who were furious at the CIA's backing of SAVAK, the Shah's blood-thirsty secret police. In revenge, the Muslims take 52 Americans hostage in the U.S. embassy in Tehran.

1979: Lebanon

CIA trains Phalangists to bomb civilians.

1979: El Salvador

An idealistic group of young military officers, repulsed by the massacre of the poor, overthrows the right-wing government. However, the US compels the inexperienced officers to include many of the old guard in key positions in their new government. Soon, things are back to "normal"—the military government is repressing and killing poor civilian protesters. Many of the young military and civilian reformers, finding themselves powerless, resign in disgust.

1980: Nicaragua

Anastasios Samoza II, the CIA-backed dictator, falls. The Marxist Sandinistas take over government, and they are initially popular because of their commitment to land and anti-poverty reform. Samoza had a murderous and hated personal army called the National Guard. Remnants of the Guard will become the Contras, who fight a CIA-backed guerilla war against the Sandinista government throughout the 1980s.

1980: El Salvador

The Archbishop of San Salvador, Oscar Romero, pleads with President Carter "Christian to Christian" to stop aiding the military government slaughtering his people. Carter refuses. Shortly afterwards, right-wing leader Roberto D'Aubuisson has Romero shot through the heart while saying Mass. The country soon dissolves into civil war, with the peasants in the hills fighting against the military government. The CIA and US Armed Forces supply the government with overwhelming military and intelligence superiority. CIA-trained death squads roam the countryside, committing atrocities like that of El Mazote in 1982, where they massacre between 700 and 1000 men, women and children. By 1992, some 63,000 Salvadorans will be killed.

1981: Iran/Contra Begins

The CIA begins selling arms to Iran at high prices, using the profits to arm the Contras fighting the Sandinista government in Nicaragua. President Reagan vows that the Sandinistas will be "pressured" until they "say 'uncle.'" The CIA's Freedom Fighter's Manual disbursed to the Contras includes instruction on economic sabotage, propaganda, extortion, bribery, blackmail, interrogation, torture, murder and political assassination.

1983: Honduras

The CIA gives Honduran military officers the Human Resource Exploitation Training Manual - 1983, which teaches how to torture people. Honduras' notorious "Battalion 316" then uses these techniques, with the CIA's full knowledge, on thousands of leftist dissidents. At least 184 are murdered.

1984: The Boland Amendment

The last of a series of Boland Amendments is passed. These amendments have reduced CIA aid to the Contras; the last one cuts it off completely. However, CIA Director William Casey is already prepared to "hand off" the operation to Colonel Oliver North, who illegally continues supplying the Contras through the CIA's informal, secret, and self-financing network. This includes "humanitarian aid" donated by Adolph Coors and William Simon, and military aid funded by Iranian arms sales.

1986: Eugene Hasenfus

Nicaragua shoots down a C-123 transport plane carrying military supplies to the Contras. The lone survivor, Eugene Hasenfus, turns out to be a CIA employee, as are the two dead pilots. The airplane belongs to Southern Air Transport, a CIA front. The incident makes a mockery of President Reagan's claims that the CIA is not illegally arming the Contras.

1987: Iran/Contra Scandal

Although the details have long been known, the Iran/Contra scandal finally captures the media's attention in 1986. Congress holds hearings, and several key figures (like Oliver North) lie under oath to protect the CIA Director William Casey who dies of brain cancer before Congress can question him. All reforms enacted by Congress after the scandals are purely cosmetic.

1988: Haiti

Rising popular revolt in Haiti means that "Baby Doc" Duvalier will remain "President for Life" only if he has a short one. The US, which hates instability in a puppet country, flies the despotic Duvalier to the South of France for a comfortable retirement. The CIA then rigs the upcoming elections in favor of another right-wing military strongman. However, violence keeps the country in political turmoil for another four years. The CIA tries to strengthen the military by creating the National Intelligence Service which suppresses popular revolt through torture and assassination.

1989: Panama

The U.S. invades Panama to overthrow a dictator of its own making, General Manuel Noriega. Noriega has been on the CIA's payroll since 1966, and has been transporting drugs with the CIA's knowledge since 1972. By the late 80s, Noriega's growing independence and intransigence have angered Washington. So out he goes.

1990: Haiti

Competing against 10 comparatively wealthy candidates, leftist priest Jean-Bertrand Aristide captures 68 percent of the vote. After only eight months in power, however, the CIA-backed military deposes him. More military dictators brutalize the country, as thousands of Haitian refugees escape the turmoil in barely seaworthy boats. As popular opinion calls for Aristide's return, the CIA begins a disinformation campaign painting the courageous priest as mentally unstable.

1993: Haiti

The chaos in Haiti grows so bad that President Clinton has no choice but to remove the Haitian military dictator, Raoul Cedras, on threat of US invasion. The US occupiers do not arrest Haiti's military leaders for crimes against humanity, but instead ensure their safety and rich retirements. Aristide is returned to power only after being forced to accept an agenda favorable to the country's ruling class.

2001: Continuous history of torture and violation of Geneva Convention.

2009–2010 Continuation under the Obama Administration of operating torture facilities in other countries.

So you see that CIA activities are not intelligence in the sense of covertly gathering information for the Executive Branch and the military to make informed decisions? What part of the government does our real intelligence work? The NSA of course, with a budget of thrice CIA's budget.

NSA Operations

For half a century, Crypto AG had sold to more than 130 countries the encryption machines their officials relied upon to exchange their most sensitive economic, diplomatic and military messages. Crypto AG was founded in 1952 by the legendary Swedish cryptographer Boris Hagelin. During World

War II, Hagelin sold 140,000 of his machine to the US Army and Navy. The machine was known as the M-209 and was used by the US Navy and Army up through the Korean War as their mainstay for encrypting messages. Ironically, it was very similar to the German Enigma machine that was the central contraption whose messages were broken in the famous drama of World War II at Bletchley Park in England. Even more ironically, the American M-209 was duplicated and broken by the Germans in a similar fashion as the Enigma, but this story is little known. There have been dozens of publications, books, newspaper stories and online exposés from the extreme that NSA owned Crypto AG to the more reasonable idea that NSA encouraged the use of Crypto AG equipment because they could easily crack any message. The story of the company Crypto AG and its continued influence from 1941 to 1990 is so central that we have to pause and give the background of Boris Hagelin.

Boris Caesar Wilhelm Hagelin was born in 1892 He was a Swedish businessman and inventor of encryption machines. He was born of Swedish parents in Georgia. Hagelin attended Lundsberg boarding school and later studied mechanical engineering at the Royal Institute of Technology in Stockholm, graduating in 1914. He gained experience in engineering through work in Sweden and the United States.

His father Karl Wilhelm Hagelin worked for Nobel in Baku, but the family returned to Sweden after the Russian revolution. Karl Wilhelm was an investor in Arvid Gerhard Damm's company, Aktiebolaget Cryptograph, established to sell rotor machines built using Damm's 1919 patent. Boris Hagelin was placed in the firm to represent the family investment. In 1925, Hagelin took over the firm, later reorganizing it as Aktiebolaget Cryptoteknik in 1932. His machines were similar to the Enigma machine made by the Scherbius Company used by Poland and Germany in World War II. The Cryptoteknik machine of Hagelins was more reliable and lower cost than the Enigma machines and actually sold much better. The two machines were very similar in concept. The Enigma machine had keys like a typewriter in contrast to the M-209 that used paper tape. The two machines competed for the contract to supply the German Wehrmacht.

At the beginning of World War II, Hagelin moved from Sweden to Switzerland, all the way across Germany and through Berlin to Geneva, carrying the design documents for the company's latest machine, and re-established his company there (it still operates as Crypto AG in Zug). That design was small, cheap and moderately secure, and he convinced the US military to adopt it. He sold 140,000 of them to the US. Hagelin became quite wealthy as a result.

After the war small countries were naturally impressed with the machine and electronic savvy of the USA and the Crypto AG products endorsed by them. They became the leading industry to supply encryption equipment to these countries. From 1949 to the late 1970s (depending on the country) the NSA routinely read their messages in real time. The world history of encryption is nothing short of naiveté. There should have been people in all these countries that knew the story of Alan Turing and his team at Bleachly Park who made the first computers to crack the Enigma. It reminds me of the time when my eight-year-old son broke his favorite record and came to me crying to glue it back together. I said OK and bought him a new one the next time I was near a record store. He went around telling everybody, "Look, my daddy glued this record back together." In addition to infiltrating Crypto AG, if they wanted to, the NSA probably had "employees" in the civilian and military ranks of most of these countries.

Figure 3.1. The M209 encryption machine. 140,000 of these were made by the US military during World War II and the Korean conflict. They were also sold to at least 130 small countries up to 1970 by AG Crypto Company of Switzerland. The encrypted message was printed out on paper tape.

After the Islamic Revolution, Iran and other Islamic countries no longer trusted equipment manufactured by companies in NATO. Iran looked to Switzerland: partly because they were not a NATO country; partly because they have a two-hundred-year reputation for neutrality; plus being world renowned for crypto equipment; and partly because the son of some Sheik took his broken record to Switzerland and someone glued it back together. So they started using Crypto AG equipment. According to Ohmy News International: *They never imagined for a moment that, attached to the encrypted message, their Crypto machines were transmitting the key allowing the descrip-*

tion of messages they were sending. The scheme was perfect, undetect-able to all but those who knew where to look.[11]

Crypto AG, of course, denied the allegations as "pure invention." On the Wikipedia page of Crypto AG, one can read: "Crypto AG rejected these accusations as pure invention, asserting in a press release that in March 1994, the Swiss Federal Prosecutor's Office initiated a wide-ranging preliminary investigation against Crypto AG, which was completed in 1997. The accusations regarding influence by third parties or manipulations, which had been repeatedly raised in the media, proved to be without foundation."

However, meetings between a NSA cryptographer and Crypto AG personnel to discuss the design of new machines have been factually established. The story was also confirmed by former employees and is supported by company documents. Boris Hagelin is said to have acted out of idealism. The story goes that the deal for Crypto AG was quite juicy. In return for rigging their machines, Crypto AG is understood to have been granted export licenses to all entities controlled by the NSA. The story is probably not true.

A book published in 1977 revealed that William F. Friedman, another Russian-born genius in the field of cryptography and one-time special assistant to the NSA director, had visited Boris Hagelin in 1957. Friedman and Hagelin met at least on two other occasions. The author was urged by the NSA not to reveal the existence of these meetings for national security reasons. The operation was codenamed the "Boris project." In effect, Friedman and Hagelin had reached an agreement that was going to pave the way to cooperation of Crypto AG with the NSA.

Of course the Iranian, Iraqis and Libyans knew none of this, even if it were true, and continued to use the Crypto AG

---

[11] http://english.ohmynews.com/ArticleView/article_view.asp?no=381337&rel_no=1

machines for all their private communications, as did dozen of other small nations. In 1987, ABC News Beirut correspondent Charles Glass was taken hostage for 62 days in Lebanon by Hezbollah, the Shi'ite Muslim group widely believed to have been founded by Ali Akbar Mohtashemi, when he was Iranian ambassador to Syria in the early 1980s.

The Arabic countries began to believe that the NSA had intercepted coded Iranian diplomatic cables between Iran's embassies in Beirut and the Hezbollah group. Iranians began to wonder how the US intelligence could have broken their code.

On July 3, 1988 the ship USS Vincennes shot down a large Iranian aircraft in the Persian Golf. Iran vowed that the skies would rain with American blood." A few months later, on Dec. 21, a terrorist bomb brought down Pan Am Flight 103 over Lockerbie, Scotland. The bombing was linked to Iran and specifically to Ali Akbar Mohtashemi, the Iranian Interior Minister. They believed that the NSA intercepted and decoded Iranian messages to give definite proof of this. This was established by intelligence summaries, prepared by the US Air Force Intelligence Agency, ware requested by lawyers for the bankrupt Pan American Airlines through the Freedom of Information Act.

Mohtashemi is closely connected with the Al Abas and Abu Nidal terrorist groups. He is actually a long-time friend of Abu Nidal. He has recently paid 10 million dollars in cash and gold to these two organizations to carry out terrorist activities and was the one who paid the same amount to bomb Pan Am Flight 103 in retaliation for the US shoot-down of the Iranian Airbus. In addition, Israeli intelligence intercepted a coded transmission between Mohtashemi in Teheran and the Iranian Embassy in Beirut concerning the transfer of a large sum of money to the Popular Front for the Liberation of Palestine-General Command, headed by Ahmed Jibril, as payment for the downing of Pan Am 103.

The Iranians then suspected that the Western Powers had possession of their keys for diplomatic traffic. If this was so, than all Iranian private messages were being compromised.

In April 1979, Shahpour Bakhtiar was forced to leave Iran as the last prime minister of the Shah. He returned to France where he lived in the west Paris suburb of Suresnes. In July 1980, he narrowly escaped an assassination attempt. On August 6, 1991, Bakhtiar and his personal secretary Katibeh Fallouch were murdered by three assassins.

Two of them fled to Iran, but the third, Ali Vakili Rad, was apprehended in Switzerland. One of the six alleged accomplices, Zeyal Sarhadi was an employee of the Iranian Embassy in Berne and a great-nephew of former president of Iran Hasemi Rafsanjani. Both men were extradited to France for trial.

On the day of his assassination and one day before his body was found with his throat slit, the Teheran headquarters of the Iranian Intelligence Service, the VEVAK, transmitted a coded message to Iranian diplomatic missions in London, Paris, Bonn and Geneva. "Is Bakhtiar dead?" the message asked. The *Neue Zurcher Zeitung*, a Swiss newspaper reported the next week that the U.S. had provided the contents of encrypted Iranian messages to France to assist investigating Magistrate Jean Louis Bruguiere in the conviction of Ali Vakili Rad and one of his alleged accomplices Massoud Hendi. This information was confirmed by *L'Expresse*.

The NSA interception and decoding of the message led to the identification of the murderers before the murder was discovered. From the Swiss and French press reports, Iranians now knew that British and American communication dragnet had intercepted and decoded the crucially embarrassing message. Something was definitely wrong with their encryption machines.

Hans Buehler was a top Crypto AG salesman who had worked at the Zug Company for 13 years. In March 1992, Buehler, a strongly-built cheerful man in his 50s, was on his 25th trip to Iran on behalf of Crypto AG. Then, on March 18, he was arrested. Iranian intelligence agents accused him of spying for the United States as well as Germany. Buehler was held in solitary confinement in the Evin prison, located in the north of Tehran. He was interrogated every day for five hours for more than nine months. "I was never beaten, but I was strapped to wooden benches and told I would be beaten. I was told Crypto AG was a spy center that worked with foreign intelligence services." Buehler never confessed any wrongdoing on his part or on the part of Crypto AG. It appeared that he had acted in good faith and the Iranians came to believe him. "I didn't know that the equipment was bugged; otherwise the Iranians would have gotten it out of me by their many methods." In January 1993, after nine months of detention, Crypto AG (or was it Siemens?) paid US$ 1 million to secure Buehler's freedom. During the first weeks after his return to Switzerland, Buehler's life was once again beautiful. The euphoria did not last long. Once more, his life came to an abrupt change. Crypto fired him and demanded repayment of the $1 million provided to Tehran for his liberation.

Back to Zug. Buehler began to ask some embarrassing questions about the Iranian allegations. And the answers tended to back up Iranian suspicions. Soon, reports began to appear on Swiss television and radio. Major Swiss newspapers and German magazines such as *Der Spiegel* picked up the story. Most, if not all, came to the conclusion that Crypto AG's equipment had been rigged by one or several Western intelligence services.

Buehler was bitterly disappointed. He felt nothing short of having been betrayed by his former employer. During all these years, Buehler never thought for a second that he had been unknowingly working for spies. Now, he was sure that he had done so. Buehler contacted several former Crypto AG employees. All admitted to him, and eventually to various media, that they believed that the company had long cooperated with US and German intelligence agencies.

One of these former engineers told Buehler that he had learned about the cooperation from Boris Hagelin Jr., the son of the company's founder and sales manager for North and South America. In the 1970s, while stranded in Buenos Aires, Boris Hagelin Jr. confided that he thought his father had been wrong to accept rigging the Crypto AG machines. Stunned by the revelation, the engineer decided to take this matter directly to the head of Crypto AG. Boris Hagelin confirmed that the encryption methods were unsafe.

"Different countries need different levels of security. The United States and other leading Western countries required completely secure communications. Such security would not be appropriate for the Third World countries that were Crypto's customers," Boris Hagelin explained to the baffled engineer. "We have to do it."

A Crypto AG official document describes an August 1975 meeting set up to demonstrate the capacity of a new prototype. The memorandum lists among the participants Nora L. Mackebee, who, like her husband, was an NSA employee. Asked about the meeting, she merely replied: "I cannot say anything about it."

During the 1970s, Motorola helped Crypto AG in making the transition from mechanical to electronic machines. Bob Newman was among the Motorola engineers working with

Crypto AG. Newman remembers very well Mackebee but says that he ignored that she was working for the NSA.

Juerg Spoerndli left Crypto AG in 1994. He helped design the machines in the late 1970s. "I was ordered to change algorithms under mysterious circumstances" to weaker machines, says Spoerndli who concluded that the NSA was ordering the design change through German intermediaries. "I was idealistic. But I adapted quickly ... the new aim was to help Big Brother USA look over these countries' shoulders. We'd say 'It's better to let the USA see what these dictators are doing'," Spoerndli says. "It's still an imperialistic approach to the world. I do not think it's the way business should be done," Spoerndli adds. Ruedi Hug, another former Crypto AG technician, also believes that the machines were rigged. "I feel betrayed. They always told me that we were the best. Our equipment is not breakable, blah, blah, blah. Switzerland is a neutral country."

Crypto AG called these allegations "old hearsay and pure invention." When Buehler began to suggest openly that there may be some truth to them, Crypto AG not only dismissed him on the spot but also filed a legal case against him. Yet Crypto AG settled the case out of court, in November 1996, before other former Crypto AG employees could provide evidence in court that was likely to have brought embarrassing details to light. No one has heard from Buehler since the settlement. "He made his fortune financially," whispers an insider.

The ownership of Crypto AG has been transferred to a company in Liechtenstein and from there back to a trust company in Munich. Crypto AG has been described as the secret daughter of Siemens but many believe that the real owner is the German government.

Several members of Crypto AG's management had worked at Siemens. At one point in time, 99.99 percent of the Crypto AG shares belonged to Eugen Freiberger, the head of the Crypto AG managing board in 1982. Josef Bauer was elected to the managing board in 1970. Bauer, as well as other members of Crypto AG management, stated that his mandate had come from the German company Siemens. The German secret service, the Bundesnachrichtendienst (BND), is believed to have established the Siemens' connection. In October 1970, a secret meeting of the BND had discussed how the Swiss company Graettner could merge with it. "The Swedish company Ericsson could be influenced through Siemens to terminate its own cryptographic business," reads the memo of the meeting. A former employee of Crypto AG reported that he had to coordinate his developments with the "central office for encryption affairs" of the BND, also known as the people from Bad Godesberg. American "watchers" demanded the use of certain encryption codes and the central office for encryption affairs instructed Crypto AG what algorithms to use to create these codes. In the industry everybody knows how such affairs will be dealt with, says a former Crypto engineer.

All of this is hearsay, from news papers and second hand sources. The important thing is that encryption machines became outdated by advances in microwave technology. From 1965 on, they were still used and were completely obsolete. The NSA and all western countries could read the private messages from Crypto AG machines in real time.

I was part of the Army Security Agency from July 1952 to July 1955. While still in the Army in January 1955 I went to graduate school full time and returned as a civilian to the NSA in July 1957. The other engineers and scientists that came to the NSA that summer are shown in the photo. They were mostly electrical engineers with a few physicists and chemists scattered among us. They were sent to graduate Electrical Engineering school at Catholic University of America until 1958 while their security clearances were being processed. That year began the biggest computer program (aka Lightning) ever funded, much bigger than all other computer programs put together.

But as far as direct attacks on foreign cryptosystems was concerned, the good news in 1957 was that solid state electronic circuits and magnetic tape storage were beginning to be reliable and faster. The NSA was frantic for higher speed circuits. This is why. As an example, consider the mechanical encryption machines used by Allied forces during World War II and the Korean conflict shown in Figure 3.1. It had six wheels for setting a session key. Each wheel had 26 letters and 10 numbers, this is 36 possible digits. There are $36^6 = 2176782336$ possible settings. If our computer and storage is fast enough to try one million keys per second, then it would take 2176 seconds or 2176/60 = 36 minutes to put the machine encrypted message into plain text. Let's say we have a key of eight digits. We have an eight digit lower case letter or number, 8 of 36 possible digits, 26 letters of the English alphabet plus 0 through 9 numerals. There are $36^8 = 2821109907456$ possible keys. If our computer and storage is fast enough to try one million keys each second, it will take about 2821109 seconds or 33 days to try all the numbers as the key. So from 1958 on a large portion of NSA personnel were involved in electronics or computers. Between 1956 and 1996 when personal computers became commonplace, we went from one million operations per second to a thousand, million (10^9) operations. So the time to find the key of 8 digits above went from 33 days in 1958 to 30 minutes in 1997. This is why starting in 1957 there was a big push to hire electrical engineers to keep up with this fast changing computing speed.

After 1958, NSA recruiters did the college rounds. Prime recruits were electrical engineers and linguists, particularly those with Chinese, Slavic, Near Eastern and Asian skills. An additional feather in a recruit's hat was knowledge of exotic languages e.g. an Indonesian dialect called Sana. Mathematicians on the M.S. or Ph.D. level were also prime.

NSA Recruits. These engineers and scientists were brought onboard NSA in the summer of 1957. The graduate electrical engineering class of Catholic University of America, they had not gone to work at NSA yet. Although being paid salary, they were waiting for clearance. FRONT, Left to Right: John Porter, Bob Brugess, Bruno Reich, Nelson McAvoy, Ray Newlin, Vince Delousa, Luther Smith, Jim Lally. CENTER, Left to Right: Bruce Middlesworth, Joseph Gray, Robert Schmidt, Donald Blouch, William Chadwell, Douglas Paden, Joseph Jepsen, Tom Mock. BACK, Left to Right: William Buckley, Joe Clark, Jack Cohn, Robert Cain, John Peaslee, James O'Neil, Herb McCoy, Robert S. Powell.

The recruiters were hamstrung by not being able to give details about the work. One aspect of working at the NSA, Fort Meade, that would have been a good sales pitch, but was never used, was that the NSA had absolutely the best employee support network of any employer on both sides of the Mississippi. I can say that unequivocally without knowing the details of other employment situations because it is so profound. Maybe partly because there is such an extensive investment in security clearances; maybe partly because they are such a highly educated work force; maybe partly because the management fosters keeping them isolated from others outside of work; maybe just happenstance; but the range of "extracurricular" activities are so vast, I think there is not a complete list and no one knows what all goes on. Are you a wine taster, a tap dancer, a Norwegian folk song enthusiast? Or would you like to herd Norwegian reindeer? Do you want to be an interlocutor or an end man in a vaudeville show and paint your face black, or would you prefer being a Shake-spearian actor? How about playing a cello in a symphony orchestra? Do you want to go skiing in a quaint villa near Quebec City or ski the Alps in Italy, Switzerland, or Austria? How about having your own duck hunting blind and a free skeet shoot to practice to your heart's content? You only have so much spare time, so you'll have to choose between making your own clothes and wrestling. Are you a theatre buff? Go to see *A Mongolian Tale* (in Mongolian, of course). You have a choice of movies in Khmer or Hausa or Welsh or Burkina Faso languages or even English. Then mosey on down to the Arundel County Yacht Club (for badge-carrying members only and their families). Join their GLOBE club (gay, lesbian or bisexual employees) or the soccer team for more active recreation. I have been told that the day care center is absolutely one of the best.

On Route I-95 between Baltimore and Washington, the ramp leading to the NSA has triple fences, armed guards, motion detectors, observation towers, the likes of a high security prison.[12] The land behind the steel-and-cement no-man's-land is a dark and mysterious place, virtually unknown to the outside world. It is made up of more than sixty buildings: offices, warehouses, factories, laboratories, and living quarters. It is a place where tens of thousands of people work in absolute secrecy. Most will live and die without ever having told their spouses exactly what they do. By the dawn of the year 2001, the Black Chamber (of 1930) had become a black empire and home to the National Security Agency, the largest, most secret, and most advanced spy organization on the planet.

Not mentioned is that the NSA has its own complete satellite system and a larger (secret) budget than the CIA, FBI and all other intelligence organizations put together.

On Friday, January 12, 1996, at 23:37:22, Pacific Standard Time, all of this changed. The NSA's main function, cryptographic intelligence, gradually diminished. There is a natural inclination not to understand that all the billions of dollars and millions of brilliant NSA scientists and mathematicians will never put "humpty dumpty back together again," i.e., code breaking is a thing of the past. People can understand the obsolescence of physical things like canals and the advances like the Global Positioning System, but not mathematical inventions. If we have to choose a date when the NSA's and everybody else's code breaking ability became obsolete, it is Friday, January 12, 1996, when the US Attorney General gave up prosecution of Phil Zimmermann for exporting a terrorist weapon, the computer freeware, PGP.

---

[12]   *Body of Secrets: Anatomy of the Ultra-Secret National Security Agency*, James Bamford. Doubleday, 2001, page 4.

Asymmetric Codes PGP and the Internet

From its beginning with telegraphy, crypto was the sole purview of the government until 1976. After World War II until 1970 there was a steady increase in the need for secret communications in the private sector. This was fueled by international banking, McCarthyism, popular resistance to the Vietnam War, the advent of computers as communications devices, and a general concern with First Amendment rights. Consequently crypto was increasingly being studied as a specialty in the mathematics departments of universities. Yet the NSA publicly, openly, and emphatically alleged that no private citizen had the right to send encrypted messages to another if the cipher was too strong for the government to break.

During the Cold War in 1959, one of the concerns of the military was that an attack on the United States would hamper our telephone links. A project was started by ARPA (Applied Research Projects Agency) to deal with this concern. ARPA was formed to eliminate the rampant duplication of applied research by the three services and civilian agencies, and did so nicely. I can vouch from personal experience as the NASA member for ARPA coordinated space-laser development. They came up with the solution that: (1) Each military and civilian center of operation of the government would have a messaging computer. (2) Messages would be typed on the computer and sent out to the appropriate recipient. (3) All messages would be divided into pieces and each piece addressed to the recipient. (4) All pieces of a message would be randomly sent to the nearest online computer and thence sent on to its destination. When all the pieces had arrived, they were assembled and printed by the recipient computer. That way, disruption of any command center would not interfere with communications to or from others. This was the beginning of the Internet which no one even dreamed of:

> In the Beginning, ARPA created the ARPANET.
> And the ARPANET was without form and void.
> And darkness was upon the deep.
> And the spirit of ARPA moved upon the face of the network and ARPA said, 'Let there be a protocol,' and there was a protocol. And ARPA saw that it was good. And ARPA said, 'Let there be more protocols,' and it was so. And ARPA saw that it was good.
> And ARPA said, 'Let there be more networks,' and it was so."
> —Danny Cohan, 1962

For example, the authors of The ARPA Completion Report (1978) wrote: Concurring about the importance of the development of e-mail, the largest single surprise of the ARPANET program has been the incredible popularity and success of network mail. There is little doubt that the techniques of network mail developed in connection with the ARPANET program are going to sweep the country and drastically change the techniques used for intercommunication in the public and private sectors.

This is a necessary background for the understanding of a need for the invention and perfection of public key cryptography. To understand why the NSA or anyone else cannot decipher encrypted messages and why public key crypto has resulted in the flourishing of Internet business, we first have to understand the RSA encryption algorithm invented in 1977[13]. The story begins with Marty Hellman. Born in 1945, his father taught physics in the New York public school system. He grew up a Jewish boy in a tough Catholic neighborhood in the Bronx. He, like me, took his refuge in math, science and ham

---

[13] *Crypto: How the Code Rebels Beat the Government—Saving Privacy in the Digital Age*, Steven Levy. Penguin, 2002.

radio and used this as an out-reach. After his Ph.D. at Stanford U. he eventually ended up there as an Assistant Professor. In 1972 enter Whitfield Diffie into his office. Diffie had called for an appointment to talk to Hellman about crypto. Whitfield Diffie was born on D-Day 1944 to a Justin Louise Whitfield and Baily Wallace Diffie. They had met while working at the US Embassy in Spain during the war. Unlike any of the other cast of characters that will bring about public key crypto, he had been absorbed in the subject from age 11. In 1965, *The Co-debreakers* by David Kahn was published. While *The Codebreak-ers* was never well known, it became a steady seller, going through dozens of printings. And it did not, as the NSA had hysterically predicted, bring an abrupt end to US intelligence. It did, however, enlighten a new generation of cryptographers who would dare to work outside of the government's wall of secrecy. And its prime student was Whitfield Diffie. By the time Whitfield Diffie finished *The Codebreakers*, he was no lon-ger depending on others to tackle the great problems of cryp-tography. He was personally, passionately engaged in them himself. They consumed his waking dreams. They were now his obsession.

Why had Diffie's once-intermittent interest become such a consuming passion? Behind every great cryptographer, it seems, there is a driving pathology. As Joseph Rochefort of the Battle of Midway fame said it, it is not necessary to be crazy to be a cryptanalysis, but it always helps. Whitfield Diffie was not crazy. Though Diffie's quest was basically an intellectual challenge, he had come to take it very personally. He had an unusual drive for getting at what he considered the bedrock truth of any issue. This lead to the fascination with protecting and uncovering secrets, especially important secrets that were desperately held. "Ostensibly, my reason for getting interested in this was its importance to personal privacy," he now says. "But I was also fascinated with investigating this business that people wouldn't tell you about," It was as if solving this conundrum would provide a more general meaning to the world at large. "I guess in a very real sense I'm a Gnostic," he said, "I had been looking all my life for some great mystery . . . I think somewhere deep in my mind is the notion that if I could learn just the right thing, I would be saved."

And then, Diffie's quest to discover truths in cryptography became intertwined with another sort of romance: His courtship of Mary Fischer. It has not been Whit Diffie's original intention to fall in love with a Jewish Brooklyn-born animal trainer who was already married. Up to the day when she upbraided him on the phone for ignoring her, he had in fact hardly thought of her. But her outburst struck a nerve, perhaps more so because his own longtime relationship was on the wane. When he bid goodbye to Mary on his way across the country, and told her he would see her in a year, he meant it. With about $12,000 he had saved from his salary at Mitre Co. and an intention to live low on the hog, as he later put it, he was out to learn all he could about crypto—and maybe do something about it. That seemed like a solitary mission.

But in August 1973, when he stopped by Fischer's New Jersey house for a visit, he found that her marriage was falling apart and that she was finding relief by going to charismatic prayer meetings. It was not the type of thing she felt comfortable talking about to mathematical types like Diffie, but when she came out with it, his reaction took her aback. "You know, Mary," he said. "I've always had a soft spot for mystics." They began to spend time together. Fischer didn't drive, and Diffie fell into the habit of escorting her to zoos—especially to locate a King cobra—and then on longer trips to view architecturally interesting churches. At one point, on a Massachusetts road, Diffie impulsively pulled the car over and very quietly told Mary he loved her. She said she loved him back. And that was that. When Diffie and Mary next drove to the West Coast for a stint of house-setting, one of the first things that Diffie did was phone this young professor of electrical engineering. "I arranged a half-hour meeting at my office at Stanford," Marty Hellman now recalls, "figuring it's just not going to go anywhere, but what the heck." Thus was made the match that, in the world of crypto, would later attain the resonance of famous pairings elsewhere: Woodward–Bernstein, Lennon–McCartney, Watson–Crick. Diffie–Hellman. The half-hour meeting went on for an hour, two hours, longer. Hellman simply didn't want it to end, and Diffie, too, seemed eager to continue for as long as possible. Hellman had promised his wife he'd be home by late afternoon to watch their two small children while she went off, so finally he asked Diffie back to his house. No problem! Diffie called Mary and she came over to have dinner with Whit and all the Hellmans; and it wasn't until 11:00 or so that night that the dialogue broke up.

Both Diffie and Hellman firmly believed that the advent of digital communications made commercial cryptography absolutely essential. All of these huge computer and telephone networks made life incredibly easy for eavesdroppers—it was going to be possible to fully automate spying. At least with radio broadcasts, snoopers had to monitor numerous points in the channel band; with a network it was as if everyone were broadcasting on the same channel. A spy agency like the NSA could—and would—simply turn on the vacuum cleaner and inhale gigabytes of data.

After a year's work together, their article *New Directions in Cryptography* made Diffie and Hellman famous. Not immediately. In fact the reaction by the old-boy network was, "Who in the hell do these whippersnappers think they are. Anyone who knows anything about cryptography knows that the most sacred and time proven thing about crypto is you have to keep your keys secret! That is what General Grant painfully learned in the Civil War. That is what the Germans painfully learned in World War II with their enigma machine. These academic types did not know that key information killed people! Diffie and Hellman knew. It was just that in 1976 the time was ripe for people in non-government domains to use crypto. But really, everyone just laughed it off. After all, there was no way to ever come up with a scheme for a public key cryptosystem.

The abstract notes that in the article "two kinds of contemporary developments in cryptography are examined. Widening applications of teleprocessing have given rise to a need for new types of cryptographic systems, which minimize the need for secure key distribution channels and supply the equivalent of a written signature. This paper suggests ways to solve these currently open problems. It also discusses how the theories of communication and computation are beginning to provide the tools to solve cryptographic problems of long standing.[14] The article goes on to say,

> We stand today on the brink of a revolution in cryptography. The development of cheap digital hardware has freed it from the design limitations of mechanical computing and brought the cost of high grade cryptographic devices down to where they can be used in such commercial applications as remote cash dispensers and computer terminals. In turn, such applications create a need for new types of cryptographic systems which minimize the necessity of secure key distribution channels and supply the equivalent of a written

---

[14] "New Directions in Cryptography", W. Diffie and M. E. Hellman, IEEE *Transactions on Information Theory*, vol. IT-22, Nov. 1976, pp. 644-654.

signature. At the same time, theoretical developments in information theory and computer science show promise of providing provable secure cryptosystems, changing this ancient art into a science. . . .

The best known cryptographic problem is that of privacy: Preventing the unauthorized extraction of information from communications over an insecure channel in order to use cryptography to insure privacy, however, it is currently necessary for the communicating parties to share a key which is known to no one else. This is done by sending the key in advance over some secure channel such as a private courier or registered mail. A private conversation between two people with no prior acquaintance is a common occurrence in business, however, and it is unrealistic to expect initial business contacts to be postponed long enough for keys to be transmitted by some physical means. The cost and delay imposed by this key distribution problem is a major barrier to the transfer of business communications through large teleprocessing networks.

Section III proposes two approaches to transmitting keying information over public (i.e., insecure) channels without compromising the security of the system. In a public key cryptosystem enciphering and deciphering are governed by distinct keys, E and D, such that computing D from E is computationally infeasible (e.g. requiring 10100 instructions). The enciphering key E can thus be publicly disclosed without compromising the deciphering key D. Each user of the network can, therefore, place his enciphering key in a public directory. This enables any user of the system to send a message to any other user enciphered in such a way that only the intended receiver is able to decipher it. A private conversation can therefore be held between any two individuals regardless of whether they have ever communicated before. Each one sends messages to the other enciphered in the receiver's public enciphering key and deciphers the message he receives using his own secret deciphering key.

> We propose some techniques for developing public
> key cryptosystems, but the problem is still largely
> open [author's emphasis, not the journal's].

The idea that you could send an encrypted message to any
stranger in the world and the stranger could be guaranteed
that it was sent by you and both you and the recipient could
be guaranteed that no one else could read it was almost ludi-
crous. The old-boy network rejected it out of hand. Anyone
who knows anything about cryptography knows that the
most sacred and time proven thing about crypto is, you have
to keep your keys secret and that identical keys have to be in
the possession of the sender and recipient. That is what General Grant painfully learned in the Civil War when he was
reprimanded by the Secretary of War. That is what the Germans painfully learned in World War II with their Enigma
machine. That is what turned the tide at the Battle of Midway
in the Pacific. These academic types did not know that key information killed people! Diffie and Hellman knew. It was just
that in 1976 the time was ripe for people in non-government
domains to use crypto. But really, everyone just laughed it off.
After all there was no way to come up with a scheme for a
public key cryptosystem!

Imagine how exciting it was when just a year later, "the
problem that was still largely open" was open no more. A
method of finding the D and E spoken of above was simple,
beautiful and functional; has been used successfully by governments, military, and business worldwide since 1980; is
used in the only software (PGP) that comes with complete
instructions (source code) to make your own software program so that you can guarantee there is no trap door; has never been compromised; has, as Diffie and Hellman predicted,
resulted in a commerce and business paradigm, called the

Internet, that will change the world in unimaginable ways in the 21st century.

It was published in 1978 by Rivest, R.; A. Shamir; L. Adleman, "A Method for Obtaining Digital Signatures and Public-Key Cryptosystems," *Communications of the ACM* 21 (2): pp.120–126. It will go down in history as one of the great documents. It is known as the RSA encryption system, after the inventors, Ron Rivest, Adi Shamir, and Leonard Adleman. They will go down in history along with other great scientific inventors such as Erwin Rudolf Josef Alexander Schrödinger, Clark Maxwell, Isaac Newton, and Albert Einstein. No small part of the RSA public key system is the "digital signatures" part of the article. Not only can one send a message completely securely, but the receiver is absolutely sure it was sent by the person who claims to be the sender. In other words, making a transaction with someone using the PGP software is as reliable as making the transaction face to face. In some ways it is even more reliable because a person can lose a credit card and a finder can take it to a store and buy everything, if the perpetrator does it before the owner cancels the card. But the most important aspect of the "digital signature" of PGP is just that; digital signature of a contract or other agreement. These days, unlike it was before all this happened, if you want to find out about any of this, you can just 'Google' these guys (or me) to your heart's content, thanks to them. You can also Google many good explanations of RSA on the net.

The algorithm is explained in detail in Appendix A. Let's first take the algorithm in its simplest form. Any one or any store that wants to receive encrypted messages has their public key published on the Internet at a key server site, such as http//keyserver.pgp.com. This is a key server that gives the public key for everyone who uses the PGP encryption software program. It is linked to the name and email address of the owner of the store. Let's suppose John Doe want to send a secure message to the Chocolate Store, to order a chocolate pig with lipstick. For simplicity we will also assume that his email messages are out there for all to intercept. His credit card number is in his order message. John Doe can look up the public key for the Chocolate Store and email the order. Of course he does not have to look up the public key on http://keyserver.pgp.com if he downloads the Chocolate Store web page; the number is embedded in their software for ordering. The public keys for the Chocolate Store are the numbers 1271 and 7. So when John Doe wants to order a chocolate pig with lipstick for $19.95 including postage, he just sends his credit card number 3521 2576 0623 1844 and address for shipping. Let's show the encryption of the first two digits, 35, of his credit card number. The RSA algorithm goes like this, $35^7 (\bmod\, 1271) = 791$ where 7 and 1271 are the public key. To get 791, go to the desktop of your PC or laptop computer and bring down the calculator. Enter 35 and then click on the $\mathbf{x}^\frown \mathbf{y}$ tab, which means x to the y power. Then enter the public key 7 and click on the = tab. Read 64339296875 as the answer. Then click on the **mod** tab and enter the other public key 1271 and read 791. 791 is sent as the encrypted 35. What this means in plane arithmetic is that you have divided 64339296875 by 1271 long division and gotten some number

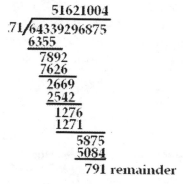

(we don't care about) and a remainder of 791.

Put in words, $35^7 (\bmod\, 1271) = 791$ means that 791 is the remainder when dividing 1271 into 35 multiplied by itself seven times. When John Doe sends out 791 for the first two digits of his credit card number, there is no way an interceptor can trace 791 back to 35 because there are a zillion numbers when divided by 1271 will give a remainder of 791. But the Chocolate Store clerk can. That makes it just as safe for John Doe as if he came to the Chocolate Store and gave them the credit card number or 'swiped' it in the Chocolate Store credit card machine. How does the Chocolate Store's computer "go backwards," i.e., decipher 791 back into 35? The Chocolate Store's computer is the only one that knows the secret key, their private key, 343. With this secret number they can go backwards, watch, $791^{343} (\bmod 1271) = 35$. Try it on your computer calculator, just as you did the encryption. Go to the desktop of your PC or laptop computer and bring down the calculator. Enter 791 and then click on the $x^{\wedge}y$ tab, which means x to the y power. Then enter 343 and click on the = tab. Read 1.18722720475381324243253 4 9208222e+994 as the answer. Then click on the **mod** tab and enter 1271 and read 35. The Chocolate Store computer does that and reads out 35 as the first two digits of John Doe's credit card number. Why is this safe? Why is it that the Chocolate Store knows the secret number 343 and no one else in the world does? Because they generated it from the RSA algorithm. It goes like this. First they chose three prime numbers. A prime is a number that cannot be evenly divided by another number. They chose, (or rather their computer chose) 31 and 41, and 7. The Chocolate Store computer multiplied 31x41=1271 and sent this and 7 out to www.pgpkeyserver.com as their public key for the rest of the world to know. These two numbers will be used by anyone who wants to order, as our example above shows. Next, how does the Chocolate Store's computer establish their private key 343? The algorithm goes like this: Subtract 1 from each of the two original prime numbers 31 and 41. 30 x 40 = 1200. We need to find k in the equation, **7(my secret number)=k(30x40)+1**. k has to be a whole number. There is a formal procedure in Appendix A for getting the lowest value of k. For this simple case, **k = 2**. Try it. 7 x 343 = 2(1200) + 1. 30 and 40 were used because they are 31-1 and 41-1. So if any message interceptors want to decipher the message 791 and get John Doe's credit card number, all they have to know is that the Chocolate Store's public key, 1271, was the product 31 x 41 = 1271, right? That is right. So the Chocolate Store uses bigger prime numbers.

We will show how this is done later, but for now let's use the Chocolate Store's public key as 1271, 7 and their private key as 343. Now let's suppose that the order for the chocolate pig with lipstick was made during the 2008 presidential election, right after vice presidential candidate Sarah Palin said in one of her speeches, "The difference between a hockey mom and a pit bull is lipstick" and presidential candidate Barack Obama remarked shortly thereafter, "You can put lipstick on a pig. It's still a pig." So the Chocolate Store gets 15,000 orders for the chocolate pig with lipstick. They send an order for more chocolate pigs to the Chocolate Factory encrypted with the Chocolate Factory's (not the Chocolate Store's) public key. They sign the order with their name, The Chocolate Store, using their private (secret) key, 343. Big deal! Yes, it is a big deal, because the Chocolate Factory can decrypt the signature using the Chocolate Store's public key. Suppose the first three digits of the number for The Chocolate Store's name are 891. The Chocolate Store encrypts 891 using their private key 343 thusly: $981^{343}=1.388255911027108154625277407887e+1026$ then click the 'mod' key on the calculator and read 847, because $981^{343} \pmod{1271}=847$. So the Chocolate Store sends the first three digits of their signature as 847. Now the Chocolate Factory knows that the first three numbers for the Chocolate Store's name is 981, as does everybody in the world. So they take the message they are sent for the Chocolate Store's signature, 847, and decrypt it using the Chocolate Store's public keys, 1271 and 7. Thus they do $847^7 = 312740317198643042863 \pmod{1271} = 981$. It was only the Chocolate Store with their secret key 343 that could have generated the number 847 that, when encrypted with the Chocolate Store's public keys 1271 and 7, could have generated 981. Voila!

Now we are back to the question, if any message inter-ceptors want to decipher the message 791 and get John Doe's credit card number, all they have to know is that the Choco-late Store's public key, 1271, was the product 31 x 41 = 1271, right? That is right. And that is easy to do because anyone would know that the two factors of 1271 are 41 and 31. So the Chocolate Store uses bigger prime numbers. For example, if the public key is 109849382951333 and 7. Now, to find the private key, what are the two primes that were multiplied together to get 109849382951333? It will take your computer a few minutes to get the two primes. They are 15426319 x 7120907 = 109849382951333. From this information one can get the private key. But what if 7 and 18819881292060796383 86972394616504398071635633794173827007633564229888 5 97152346654853190606065047430453173880113033967161 99 69232120573403187955065699622130516875930765025705 9 are the public keys? Now how long will it take a hacker or NSA computer to find the two primes, when multiplied to-gether, gives you this number? It will take months using the best and fastest computer. But my computer at the Chocolate Factory multiplied two primes together and got this number in no time. And so if someone wants to find the first two digits of John Doe's credit card number 35, it will take them a month for a dedicated computer. It is just not worth the trouble to find out what the two primes were that the Chocolate Factory used to generate their public key. Don't spend months trying different primes to find out, I'll tell you. One was,

39807508642406493739712550055038649119906436234 252670840638518957594638895726176858317

and the other was,

47277214610743530253622307197304822463291469530209711645985217113052071125636359039752 7.

This is the essence of public key crypto. It takes a long time to factor two prime numbers that can be multiplied together in no time. Copy and paste these two prime numbers into your desktop calculator and see if you don't get the public key number above: 18819881292060796383869723946165043980716356337941738270076335642298885971523466548531906060650474304531738801130339671619969232120573403187955065699622130516875930765025705 9. Note that it took your calculator only a small fraction of a second to do this multiplication. These two primes are about 32 digits long. Count them and you will see. There are about 135717025594766196140977787161 4 primes smaller than these two. For round numbers lets say there are 10^{30} respectable size primes smaller than these. Let's say the very, very fastest computer could try a million, million, million, of these primes every second, i.e. 10^{18} primes could be tried per second. How long would it take to try them all? It would take $10^{30}/10^{18} = 10^{12}$ **seconds**. This is many thousands of years.

This is the essence of public key crypto. It takes a long time to factor two prime numbers that can be multiplied together pronto. It is the same idea as, how long would it take to mix a glass of milk and a glass of ink? A lot less time than it would take to separate the mix back to where you could drink the milk. Maybe you say, "Well the NSA has many of the fastest computers in the world." Look up Nelson McA-

voy's public key on http://www.pgpkeyserver.com and you
will see that it is:

10981697866698054841021156667656871109558078547874431071057470477610912012211648103791009011898695267114547410811710283551218267907010710051561081225089113497949516612167809882759847738211098734888531101104953881089990117108100547383120791007511872108534889558469694855817411677551081155073109861117753108708786112507955901008254118501204810451671081038411411610410910097701055250109122114545011652894949537610711551807911352855367105826756107971037968117119486647811031016688118118698811981864811211511210478671005149109109109828611512178119555410211611010910078567911911911687109678652120771185312011610355821031101117711999111817973491051031007911649117117716674534712011777567010380825766120103122721121151149752120108511201017466119671011048549118120671168082105109689010771115874386857884551067452117120109849910684871121114984103691051084910210368656669666565714875107531089872781189810566788948705098511071038072100108891094910499518210899107665398518648976749122985078106908873117895057116801111076673103818165817365686585678366746690658568656674496565657567826788697610598121108101116102758297664752511171025610687674768119805450113106103117108671211104998611511145610210786887349521076511111181008580908556979768501201081211187877507557116113678011511199109768611755113571048011490118102105731089810052881221007156701078379117113102113105104561161051041201225453438555438411565671111065711782103891184975841067311475101848310579791004310976564785471115486735372898180112103738412081991201161111171016510476103108864790527372841204910910777104739780801061081171149810112183

49679973557110343821151021031041128087121724997991155248569910855761071091131021077849537710243506810985121881161224810686821141051025110279496982685410975508397112100837480787867677485651021171211079772791076711311355118471121036843551077111871101113531085212073100118888584114122975743100491218512270498912143112103115105117696784515683119481085583435710581717266666566651036612066817474906799707766836565656565656567656566516612190879010899110741089067491089887701129867491089810978118907110811790486611990516511789505711699711001199887108116908199766781103726511973756510410766718210411100728211979105561189750865399508612110010986121761106611099675310698504870711197765656565687010373666682526665656566666857367811116567103107814869118122795511188551136811710610310365113113112791117610211052896911875684367116737411547808610599103899711888117556811781110796710276777097831088810365898598528810684671068456112805469771089899561104310648103791168110943981191061055711590567567471171037450118565511956120801129910872101728751495447104815212186988411112268719779108661061161181051195711571101067882878185978911211990107431018653825211088711041147343721191219010799119116987511611754100115101904770834910911797561011025712148541055469725266864965100538054688783112777411987671121111141161111207610752558097695299518972120895110110074531035280811088555971145543106113117751227048114101109113508810312111966849790505510511268861108911787711178872119775611410754501138882514956437754488912074108121100541078076701171041157810766687511489887910288875110373908356505575847811611399885276107666881826843107515565811036549671218671434385561225710311881116489982116671178710412210647107908310555477672481125 78

71197810810210110766868774119825757100537070901048910647111674875811185270511111081218398715049905777515049105691144710474103100725275565478706948531091081188988471216775439976717471118118904866121112861191147610448699710768791018677805355431108550844849891185554521071104871721091141111228797485678678353977053121118861068576521088677549865525588100809965801228957116100831117910543751156878117102666590755087109120486673568771114120761106810043507969798710153851131201057643744810912078544311910098904989654870768587103817482991145590568411450728665711026570731006911811210981726657674711511698103667411478101120654771797757527349110828082113508111911478106725272105100117707267501181217811175527711965826581656610581746666661036665103691146681747097110119886682115776565656511970481036666107666765657166817470971101198765651117469796948908590109112905353999711572471051151157312211211612168765211598556689988010650121103791008711073488910910649711027869841171097611189871181135084434372701017311248501095471781208983105671201178498875510351787710365718286729088121120898699997755535665113117748575110841204385741179880671201071026710597101891187484666555487810197110531051025211648537011655122571077812076115498212154118108821195354781218985108551138110311010011710511079655778688599731055311286976910254541197748117104541228975668877122898252112547410098741047849476748111481061096583120116721181031131058078721140 ——END PGP PUBLIC KEY BLOCK——

This key is about 4680 (binary) digits long. It is the product of two prime numbers. The NSA was bragging to James Bamford at one of his interviews that they could do a million, million, million, million (10^{24}) operation a second with their super computers. To find out the two primes used in my public key, it would only take NSA 10^{180} years. So go ask your congressman, "Can the NSA ever decrypt a message sent by PGP with an RSA public key of 2048 bit?" Or, "Congressman, do you think the terrorists up in the hills of Afghanistan, or sitting at an outdoor cafe in Washington DC, are too stupid to use encryption with a 2048 bit key?" Or better still, "Congressman, since the NSA or anyone else can never decrypt email in less than a few thousand years, don't you think that they, like all other government agencies, should have congressional oversight?" Don't waste your breath, I'll tell you what he will say. He'll say, "Well, you know, you never know what technology will bring. Maybe they can break codes and, of course, they would not tell anybody." But Congressman, in 1997 William Crowell, Deputy Director of NSA, said that "*If all the personal computers in the world—260 million—were put to work on a single PGP-encrypted message, it would still take an estimated 12 million times the age of the universe, on average, to break a single message.*" The Congressman will say, "Well, if they can decipher messages, they wouldn't admit it, would they?" The congressman gets away with this because the public, the news analysis, and people in general do not trust a mathematical analysis. Probably in a generation or so, after billions of email messages have been successfully sent and received securely, people will begin to trust the process. Remember what George Lakoff and the cognitive scientists are saying, "Our common sense is what we see and hear over and over again as we grow up." So maybe the next generation of congressmen will know better.

Enter now the sixth and last of the main contributors to what is now common place computer software for worldwide message privacy—the folk hero, the Tom Paine of the 20th century, Phil Zimmermann. From 1980 to 1995 the NSA did everything in its power to destroy Phil Zimmermann's invention of a software package that was free-ware and compatible with the mushrooming use of personal computers. The story is much more exciting than any fiction and is detailed in *Crypto*.[15] This story ends in 2007 by which time most personal computers and laptops were coming new with Phil Zimmermann's PGP software installed for personal private communications. It is also used for the most sensitive of messages inter and intra governments.

Phil Zimmermann, like Whitfield Diffie, was interested in crypto at an early age. Unlike Whitfield Diffie, he was not born with a silver spoon in his mouth. Born in 1954, his father was a truck driver. Both his father and mother were alcoholics. As a fourth grader, he watched a TV show called *M.T. Graves and the Dungeon*. If a fan sent in money, he would get the key to decipher a secret message used in the adventures of *M.T. Graves*. Phil needed no key. He would bust the cipher wide open. As is usually the case, his interest in things academic, and in his case crypto, waned in his teenage years. Then, as a student at Florida Atlantic University, where he was a computer science major, he realized that the computer was just the thing for breaking codes. In those days, the proliferation of computers for business inventories and bookkeeping meant that jobs for graduates in this field were plentiful. What a bonanza for a boy who had struggled so hard. As an employee of a minicomputer company in Fort Lauderdale, Phil Zimmermann came across an article in *Scientific American*, August 1977,[16] that spread the word about the newly invented RSA crypto system:

The upward creep of postal rates accompanied by the deterioration of postal service is a trend that may or may not continue, but as far as most private communication is con-

---

[15] *Crypto*, ibid.

[16] *Scientific American*, "A New Kind of Cipher That Would Take Millions of Years to Break," Martin Gardner, pages 120-125.

cerned, in a few decades it probably will not matter. The reason is simple. The transfer of information will probably be much faster and much cheaper by "electronic mail" than by conventional postal systems. Before long it should be possible to go to any telephone, insert a message into an attachment and dial a number. The telephone at the other end will print out the message at once.

Government agencies and large business will presumably be the first to make extensive use of electronic mail, followed by small businesses and private individuals. When this starts to happen it will become increasingly desirable to have fast, efficient ciphers to safeguard information from electronic eavesdroppers. A similar problem is involved in protecting private information stored in computer memory banks from snoopers who have access to the memory through date-processing networks.

It is hardly surprising that in recent years a number of mathematicians have asked themselves: Is it possible to devise a cipher that can be rapidly encoded and decoded by computer, can be used repeatedly without changing the key and is unbreakable by sophisticated cryptanalysis? The surprising answer is yes. The breakthrough is scarcely two years old, yet it bids fair to revolutionize the entire field of secret communication. Indeed, it is so revolutionary that all previous ciphers, together with the techniques for cracking them, may soon fade into oblivion. . ."

Leonard Adleman found out in short order the impact of this article. He was in his old stomping grounds in Berkeley, California. At the checkout counter, the customer in front of him said to the other customer in line, who was buying *Scientific American*, "Did you see the thing in here about the new code system?" "Yeah, I read about it. Isn't it wild?" When Len said he was one of the authors, the clerk rolled his eyes. But they were easy to convince. "Would you sign this for me?" the clerk asked. From then on, the three young professors from MIT's Academic Square were celebrities around the cerebral world.

And what was the reaction inside the Fort George Meade, Maryland, intelligence bastion? The top echelon was stunned into denial for a while and it took the rank and file a month or so to see what had happened. Down the road about 15 miles from Fort Meade, at Goddard Space Flight Center, I was the Head Scientist for space-to-space laser communications. When I read the article, I remember that I had to lay it on the table and read it. I couldn't hold it, my hands were shaking too much.

I don't know if Phil Zimmermann's hands were shaking but he was probably much more excited than I was. He immediately called Ron Rivest at MIT and a long conversation followed regarding the implementing of RSA on a computer. Ron told him that they were already doing that on a grandiose scale at MIT. It was a natural for anyone in the new field of personal computers and/or crypto to see a software program for email security. Between 1978 and 1992 there were extensive efforts in this area. The three RSA inventors used their MIT patent to form a company, RSA Security, Inc. The company intended to license public key for the kind of system that Phil Zimmermann thought only he was pioneering.

Charles Merritt, a programmer who set up a company in Fayetteville, Arkansas, was doing what Phil Zimmermann had been working on and dreaming of for years. Merritt actually was selling RSA encryption systems to small foreign nations and large companies.

Phil Zimmermann formed a company called Metamorphic Systems. Metamorphic Systems' business waned as the Apple II got squeezed out by IBM dominance. "But everything

changed (for Phil) with a single phone call from a programmer in Arkansas who had a scheme few people could appreciate more than Phil Zimmermann. The guy's name was Charlie Merritt, and it turned out that he was actually doing the
thing that Zimmermann had dreamed of since reading Martin Gardner's column in 1977: he was implementing an RSA
public key cryptosystem in a microcomputer. Merritt had
experienced a similar reaction to Zimmermann's when he'd
read about the work of the MIT researchers. Moving from his
native Houston, Texas, to Fayetteville, Arkansas, he started
a company with several friends and they actually managed
to create a public key program running on Z-80 computers.
It ran very slowly, but worked. But no one seemed to want
to buy it. After a while, his friends dropped out, and Merritt
with his wife Hobbit began selling the program themselves.
Eventually news of their tiny enterprise reached the intelligence operation in Fort Meade. Periodically the NSA would
send its representatives to Arkansas to warn Merritt of the
dire consequences that might ensue if he sent any encryption
packages out of the country. Since Merritt Software's customers were large oversees companies that wanted encryption to circumvent the peeping thugs of corrupt regimes, this
restriction virtually shut the company down. To try to get
some domestic leads, Merritt was reduced to calling obscure
companies he'd read about in computer magazines, hoping
they would package his program with their stuff. That was
how he found Metamorphic and Phil Zimmermann. When
Zimmermann heard what Merritt was up to, his excitement
was so over the top that Merritt suspected a practical joke
was being played on him.

Merritt and Zimmermann became so entwined that the
families had a week long two-man conference in Boulder,
Colorado in November 1986. Three-man, actually, because

Charlie invited Jim Bidzos, the CEO of RSA Securities, Inc. Bidzos brought with him a copy of Mailsafe, a program written by Rivest and Adleman of RSA fame. There are as many different versions of what transpired at the meeting as there were attendants. When Phil finished his PGP program He named it after an advertising farce skit on the Garrison Keller's Prairie Home Companion radio show, Pretty Good Groceries. He had used the RSA algorithm that was patented and needed licensing. He did not have a license and there was a corporate donnybrook over this that was to be worked out before PGP could be sold to customers. But it was all moot, thanks to Senator Joe Biden, head of the Senate Intelligence Committee. Maintaining his reputation for stirring up a bee's hive with good intentions, he inserted a paragraph in Senate Bill 266 draft on January 23, 1991 to wit:

> "It is the sense of Congress that providers of electronic communications services and manufacturers of electronic communications service equipment shall ensure that communications systems permit the government to obtain the plaintext contents of voice, data, and other communications when appropriately authorized by law."

That did it. The Internet crypto guys found out about this language in Bill 266 in April. Kelly Goen, a friend of Charlie Merritt and Zimmermann, according to an article in the *Micro Times* by Jim Warren. "He [Goen] was driving around the Bay Area with a laptop, acoustic coupler, and cellular phone. He would stop at a pay phone, upload a number of copies for a few minutes, then disconnect and rush off to another phone miles away. He said he wanted to get as many copies scattered as widely as possible around the nation before the government could get an injunction and stop him." Of course Kelly Goen made sure that the sites to whom he uploaded were in the US. The next day thousands and thousands of people all over the world had downloaded PGP from the bulletin board and were encrypting email to each other. At that time it was a particularly big boon to the freedom fighters in Estonia and Lithuania in their efforts to breakaway from the USSR. By doing this Phil Zimmermann gave up a livelihood potential that he had been working toward for 12 years. Because he was giving the software away and not selling it, he overcame the licensing problem with RSA Security Inc. By spreading around freeware, he also defeated the government's efforts to restrict crypto. As a result he was under indictment for three years for the felony charges of exporting a terrorist weapon.

But in the end he was exonerated as these emails show.

Date: Fri, 12 Jan 1996 23:37:22 -0700
From: "Philip L. Dubois"
Subject: News Release
"Yesterday morning, I received word from Assistant U.S. Attorney William Keane in San Jose, California, that the government's three-year investigation of Philip Zimmermann is over. Here is the text of Mr. Keane's letter to me:"
"The U.S. Attorney's Office for the Northern District of California has decided that your client, Philip Zimmermann, will not be prosecuted in connection with the posting to USENET in June 1991 of the encryption program Pretty Good Privacy. The investigation is closed."
The U.S. Attorney also released this to the press:
"Michael J. Yamaguchi, United States Attorney for the Northern District of California, announced today that his office has declined prosecution of any individuals in connection with the posting to USENET in June 1991 of the encryption program known as "Pretty Good Privacy." The investigation has been closed. No further comment will be made by the U.S. Attorney's Office on the reasons for declination.

Assistant U.S. Attorney William P. Keane of the U.S. Attorney's Office in San Jose at (408) 535-5053 oversaw the government's investigation of the case."

On receiving this news, Mr. Zimmermann posted this to the Cypherpunks list:

My lead defense lawyer, Phil Dubois, received a fax this morning from the Assistant US Attorney in Northern District of California, William Keane. The letter informed us that I "will not be prosecuted in connection with the posting to USENET in June 1991 of the encryption program Pretty Good Privacy. The investigation is closed."

This brings to a close a criminal investigation that has spanned the last three years. I'd like to thank all the people who helped us in this case, especially all the donors to my legal defense fund. Apparently, the money was well-spent. And I'd like to thank my very capable defense team: Phil Dubois, Ken Bass, Eben Moglen, Curt Karnow, Tom Nolan, and Bob Corn-Revere. Most of the time they spent on the case was pro bono. I'd also like to thank Joe Burton, counsel for the co-defendant. There are many others I can thank, but I don't have the presence of mind to list them all here at this moment. The medium of email cannot express how I feel about this turn of events.

Philip Zimmermann

11 Jan 96

Phil Dubois later that day wrote:

I'd like to add a few words to those of my client. First, I thank Mr. Keane for his professionalism in notifying us of the government's decision. It has become common practice for federal prosecutors to refuse to tell targets of investigations that the government has decided not to prosecute. I appreciate Mr. Keane's courtesy.

... These lawyers are heroes. They donated hundreds of hours of time to this cause. Each is outstanding in his field and made a contribution that nobody else could have made. It has been an honor and a privilege to work with these gentlemen....

Those members of the press who recognized the importance of this story and told the world about it should be commended. Undeterred by the absence of sex and violence, these reporters discussed the real issues and in so doing served the public well.

...

Now, some words about the case and the future. Nobody should conclude that it is now legal to export cryptographic software. It isn't. The law may change, but for now, you'll probably be prosecuted if you break it. People wonder why the government declined prosecution, especially since the government isn't saying. One perfectly good reason might be that Mr. Zimmermann did not break the law. (This is not always a deterrent to indictment. Sometimes the government isn't sure whether someone's conduct is illegal and so prosecutes that person to find out.) Another might be that the government did not want to risk a judicial finding that posting cryptographic software on a site in the U.S., even if it's an Internet site, is not an "export." There was also the risk that the export-control law would be declared unconstitutional. Perhaps the government did not want to get into a public argument about some important policy issues: should it be illegal to export cryptographic software? Should U.S. citizens have access to technology that permits private communication? And ultimately, do U.S. citizens have the right to communicate in absolute privacy?

There are forces at work that will, if unresisted, take from us our liberties. There always will be. But at least in the United States, our rights are not so much stolen from us as they are simply lost by us. The price of freedom is not only vigilance but also participation. Those folks I mention in this message have participated and

no doubt will continue. My thanks and the thanks of
Philip Zimmermann, to each of you.

Phil Zimmermann did not export PGP to other countries.
He put it on the "bulletin board." One of the new concepts
that the prosecution would have to face in a Phil Zimmermann trial is, what constitutes exporting? As they say, on the
Internet, national boundaries are just speed bumps.

Chapter 4. NSA 1997–2010

Five months after the Attorney General had announced that they would not prosecute Phil Zimmermann for exporting a terrorist weapon, the Subcommittee on Science, Technology, and Space of the US Senate Committee on Commerce, Science, and Transportation heard this testimony of Philip R. Zimmermann to on 26 June 1996:

> . . . . I wrote PGP from information in the open literature, putting it into a convenient package that everyone can use in a desktop or palmtop computer. Then I gave it away for free, for the good of democracy. This could have popped up anywhere, and spread. Other people could have and would have done it. And are doing it. Again and again. All over the planet. This technology belongs to everybody.
> PGP has spread like a prairie fire, fanned by countless people who fervently want their privacy restored in the information age.

Today, human rights organizations are using PGP to protect their people overseas. Amnesty International uses it. The human rights group in the American Association for the Advancement of Science uses it. It is used to protect witnesses who report human rights abuses in the Balkans, in Burma, in Guatemala, in Tibet. Some Americans don't understand why I should be this concerned about the power of government. But talking to people in Eastern Europe, you don't have to explain it to them. They already get it— and they don't understand why we don't.

I want to read you a quote from some E-mail I got in October 1993 from someone in Latvia, on the day that Boris Yeltsin was shelling his own Parliament building: "Phil I wish you to know. Let it never be, but if dictatorship takes over Russia your PGP is widespread from Baltic to Far East now and will help democratic people if necessary. Thanks."

Major changes in the intelligence activities around the world took place gradually between 1997 and September 11, 2001: After 1997, private and national entities (including the NSA) were no longer in the code breaking business. PGP was freeware and secure. There has not been a case of a PGP message being broken with the commonly used 1024 bit keys in the last 25 years. Even the US and British governments have adapted PGP for use by military and other branches. PGP is now used by banks and terrorist groups alike. A red herring is that when computers become faster, keys can be found more quickly. This is not true because with faster computers, keys can be proportionally bigger. Because it was put on the Internet as freeware, PGP had the advantage that it was available to every Tom, Dick, and Harry even before it was included with browsers.

The world has seen the proliferation of desperate people who strap explosives on their bodies, and commit suicide, taking from thousands to dozens of bystanders with them. The NSA with their experts in the language, culture, history, dress, and customs of hundreds of nations and tribes, is uniquely equipped to combat them. Their most valuable role has shifted from COMINT to HUMINT. They are additionally well equipped for their new emphasis in human intelligence by having been out of the limelight since their inception.

As an example of the misunderstanding and continued deception of Congress and the people about the United States intelligence operations, I give a few lines from the Charlie Rose TV show, January 14, 2010. He is interviewing a journalist about the CIA[17]:

> We begin tonight with an ongoing look at the United States intelligence community. Over the weekend CIA Director Leon Panetta publicly defended his agent industry from criticism over last month's suicide attack in Afghanistan that killed seven of his employees. In an editorial in the *Washington Post*, Panetta dismissed claims that agents had practiced poor trade craft. The public defense came days after President Obama acknowledged security missteps that led to Al Qaeda's attempt to bring down a U.S. airliner on Christmas Day.
> In addition, the military's highest-ranking intelligence officer in Afghanistan released a critical self-assessment last week. Major General Michael Flynn wrote that "analysis was unable to understand and answer fundamental questions about the war."
> Joining me now from Washington is David Ignatius, a columnist for the *Washington Post*. He often covers the intelligence community and writes novels about it. In Berkeley, California, is Bob Baer, former CIA officer. And in New York, Mark Mazzetti of the *New York Times*. He covers national security issues for the newspaper.

[17] www.charlierose.com/guest/view/465/

David, you and I have had many conversations about the CIA and about CIA activities, including ...what's often based on things that you know from real life. Tell me what we now know about what happened in Afghanistan to those CIA agents and what we now know about the Al Qaeda operative and how he fooled so many people.

To paraphrase David Ignatius:

Although the CIA, Charlie, is putting together all the details of this, right now they have a fairly clear picture. This was typical deceptive use of double agents. This Jordanian, al-Balawi, was a well known Internet icon as an Islamic radical. He was arrested by the Jordanian intelligence service. We thought that the Jordanians had turned him. That he was turned to become a double agent. We thought he was sent into Pakistan by the Jordanians and he was sending them, and CIA through them, valuable information. . . . When he came to the CIA base in eastern Afghanistan, that is Khost, it was like a large reception committee for a dignitary. Except for one Jordanian, they were all American CIA operatives. They were all waiting in anticipation that this one double agent would provide for the necessary arrangement for assassination of top drawer Al Qaeda officials, especially the number two man, Ayman al-Zawahiri. The waiting entourage were mostly killed.

Dr. Humam Khalil Abu-Mulal al-Balawi blew himself up and took 11 CIA operatives with him.... What is disturbing as you look at this, I think, are two things. First, the breakdown in basic trade craft, the basic ways in which the CIA tries to secure itself against the dangers of this kind of double agent who turns

Dr. al-Balawi

out to be a triple agent coming back against you. And, secondly, what it shows us about the sophistication of Al Qaeda....

An important statement by Mark Mazzetti was:

And, as both David and Bob said, this was, you know, a guy who could maybe deliver the mother lode. He could get them al-Zawahiri and maybe bin Laden. So you saw this eagerness to make this happen.

Another important statement in the half-hour long conversation, by Bob Baer, was:

And what struck me at Khost—I think I know almost everybody there. There were no Pashtun speakers or even Dari speakers. And in that part of Afghanistan, if you don't speak the language, it's virtually impossible to get to the populace. And the military I've seen internally is complaining that most of their foreign-language specialists speak Dar rather than Pashtun, which—you know, this is same problem the British had in the three wars they fought in Afghanistan. They had very few Pashtun speakers.

As William Shakespeare said, Oh what tangled web we weave when we fashion to deceive. What is the deception to the American people here? These CIA operatives were not into intelligence, they were into assassination.

Mark Mazzetti let the cat out of the bag with the above quote. These CIA operative in their enclaves in Khost, Afghanistan, have the job of killing top-drawer Al Qaeda figures. If the CIAs kill al-Zawahiri, big deal, so we make them mad and maybe an even more capable zealot will take his place. They are not gathering intelligence.

The United States intelligence services have men and women of all walks of life in Jordan and Palestine and Afghanistan who speak all dialects. If this were about gathering information, the US intelligence apparatus would make surreptitious contact with Dr. al-Balawi. They also have all kinds of sophisticated methods for Dr. al-Balawi to communicate with his handlers, if he wanted to be a double. They would never want him near the Khost center, never, ever. Openly drive in a car with the King of Jordan's cousin to the CIA enclave!

Charlie Rose is one example of the misconception of the CIA as an intelligence agency. Who is supposed to find out where and how much and by whom poppy is grown in Afghanistan? Who buys it? How is it refined? Where is it shipped? That's what intelligence is. You can be sure we have intelligence agents in Afghanistan. They are not in an air-conditioned enclave in Khost. They are hot in the summer and cold in the winter. They blend in with the local people. Some are US citizens. Some have joined the US army with the guarantee that their "time in grade" as a "green card" holder will be shortened by a stint in Afghanistan. Some are just 'kids' who joined the NSA when they got out of college and had a concentrated learning experience in Afghanistan culture, language, customs, songs, et cetera. Without infiltrating, we have nothing. You see why the NSA does not want Congressional oversight? You see why they do not want to take the risk of some blabber mouth stupid Congressman jeopardizing the life of their 'kids'. We owe it to these agents who infiltrate, to keep them safe. You see why they want the Charlie Roses and David Ignatiuses and all of us to think that CIA does intelligence work? Now let me tell you a story about how intelligence really works. I don't have any examples from present day NSA activities but will go back to a story that I lived. In the beginning of Chapter 3, I talked about a quote by General Harry Reicheldorfer the Arlington Hall Commandant. I can remember this quote, "In other words, gentlemen, CIA is not an intelligence agency; NSA will be this country's intelligence agency. I repeat, this conflict in Korea and our hostility with the USSR has taught us that we no longer productively separate COMINT and HUMINT."

One NSA project that I carried out between 1958 and 1961 is a good explanation of why COMINT and HUMINT cannot be separated. During this time microwave receivers were notoriously of poor quality. Signals had to be strong to be intercepted. The research effort at the NSA had two main thrusts. One was faster computers and the other was more sensitive radio receivers in the microwave spectrum. One band of interest was the 1420 MHz band (wavelength of 21 cm). This band was used for fighter-to-fighter talk between pilots of USSR MIGs. These signals were for short distance and line-of-sight and so were very weak. The Berlin Blockade from June 1948 to May 1949 was one of the first major international crises of the Cold War. During the multinational occupation of post-World War II Germany, the Soviet Union blocked the Western Allies' railway and road access to the sectors of Berlin under their control. Their aim was to force the western powers to allow the Soviet zone to start supplying Berlin with food and fuel, thereby giving the Soviets practical control over the entire city.

In response, the Western Allies organized the Berlin Airlift to carry supplies to the people in West Berlin. Over 4,000 tons per day was required by Berlin during the airlift. Commonwealth nations, and the United States Air Force, flew over 200,000 flights providing 13,000,000 tons of food to Berlin in an operation lasting almost a year. By the spring of 1949, the effort was clearly succeeding, and by April the airlift was delivering more cargo than had previously flowed into the city by rail. MIG fighters were constantly harassing the airlift planes. The NSA frantically needed a sensitive receiver in the 21 cm band.

This also happened to be the wavelength of glowing hydrogen from distant galaxies. Of course the existence of hydrogen in other planets is a dead give away to the postulate of life thereon.

Enter on the stage next Eugene Fubini. His obituary in 1997 mentioned that: His duties as deputy director of research and engineering included overseeing the National Security Agency, the ultra-secret organization with the missions of devising and breaking codes and operating an electronic espionage network. In 1937 Gene's life changed drastically. For one, he lost his dear friend and mentor Guglielmo Marconi. He always teared up when talking about the exciting days of the invention of radio. For another, that year his family immigrated to the US. His father was a mathematics professor in Italy and got out from under Mussolini to join the Institute for Advanced Study in Princeton, N.J. In 1958 Eugene Fubini was the principle engineer at Airborne Instrument Laboratory on Long Island. He worked closely with Robert O. Alde, the director of research (RADE) at the NSA.

Bob was a very methodical and informal guy who always put people at ease. He used to shock me by raking a bunch of top-secret papers into something between a suitcase and a brief case and saying, "Let's go." He didn't make reservations on a plane; he just went to the airport and bought a ticket and went from one company to another. Then, sleeping in his rumpled suit, he decided where he would go next. He took me to Long Island one day and just left me there with Eugene Fubini and Matthew Ladenbalm. Fubini had a half-dozen little bambinos in a hallway-like waiting room. It ended up that he was busy and there were wall-to-wall kids: we played cowboys-and-Indians all over the place. The next day, Dr. Fubini and I had a long talk and here comes Bob Alde back in the same old rumpled suit. He said, "We're off to Boston." Off we went. He bought my ticket; I didn't have much money with me and of course we didn't have credit cards then.

We went to the office of the director of Lincoln Laboratory, a research institute of Massachusetts Institute of Technology. He blew my mind. He told them I was from West Virginia and would be working at the radio astronomy telescope in Green Bank, WV (receiving hydrogen-line radio signals). The fact that I was from West Virginia University wasn't involved in their choice of picking someone for the job; it just made the cover story almost nonexistent. They brought in Stanley H. Autler and told him that the two of us would be working on making a low-noise amplifier for the 1420 MHz hydrogen line, implying that I was to be his step-and-fetch-it. He had been a graduate student under Charles Towns, the original inventor of the idea of lasers and the original ammonia maser and later a Nobel Laureate. A year or so later we published a report.[18] A regenerative solid-state maser has been constructed for 1420 MHz using 0.05% Cr^{+++} in $K3Co(CN)6$ and a pump frequency of 3850 MHz. A magnetic field of 480 Oe at 11° to the crystalline a-axis in the ac-plane the 1–2 transition was used for the signal frequency and the 1–3 transition for the pump frequency; numbering the levels in order of increasing energy. The product of voltage gain and bandwidth was 2.7×10^6s-1.

The only practical catch was that it only worked at -450°F! We commonly say 4 degrees Absolute, 4 degrees above the temperature where all molecular motion stops. This was not a problem in the laboratory. You just put it down in a thermos bottle about 3 feet long. The thermos bottle had another ther-

---

[18] "21-Centimeter Solid-State Maser," Phys. Rev. 110, 280–281 (1958), Stanley Autler and Nelson McAvoy.

mos bottle around it. In the inside thermos bottle you poured liquid helium. It boils at 4 degrees Absolute. The outside thermos was filled with liquid nitrogen; it boils at 70 degrees Absolute. It will last about 21 hours if you don't shake it up too much. It was a room full of equipment.

Now, back to the Berlin Airlift. As previously explained, we were reading USSR traffic during the 1948 airlift but it soon dried up. In 1958, we knew the USSR was making plans for some big move, but we did not know exactly what. It was the Wall. Before the Wall's erection, 3.5 million East Germans had avoided Eastern Bloc emigration restrictions and defected from the Eastern Bloc. Eastern Bloc people could easily travel to Berlin. West Berlin was really an island in the Eastern Bloc. Many came to Berlin from the USSR, even Asia, and Eastern Europe, then crossed over from East Berlin into West Berlin. From West Berlin, they could travel to West Germany and other Western European countries. Western airlines had regular commercial flights out of Tempelhof Airport in West Berlin. During its existence from 1961 to 1989, the Wall stopped almost all such immigration and separated the Eastern Bloc from West Berlin for more than a quarter of a century. In 1958 most NSA analysts thought that the USSR would simply abolish the West Berlin 'island,' a very straightforward and irrecoverable act. Robert O. Alde did not believe this. In his calm way he was desperately making plans to know every little move of the Russians with regard to Berlin. He at Fort Meade and Eugene Fubini at Airborne Instrument Laboratory on Long Island, and others, were working urgently for 'ears and agents' in Berlin. Incidentally, when the Wall went up, Bob Alde said, "This is the best thing that could happen for the West in this Cold War." Everyone around laughed in a ridiculing way (including me; sorry, Bob); and that was the only time I ever saw him have a look of irritation. He was right. The Wall brought out a contrast between East and West that would not have been obvious otherwise.

So I moved back to Fort Meade and built the most reliable and field worthy 1420 MHz maser on both sides of the Mississippi. It was a monster; it reminded me of the Frankenstein movie gadgets. I quit working at the NSA and went to NASA, Goddard Space Flight Center, down the road. It was not long before Bob Alde called and said, "Let's go."

It was not until I came back from that trip and thought about it that I realized the extent to which it had been choreographed. A whole section had taken over my maser at Fort Meade, honchoed by Bobby Walker. They tested, improved and had it broken down and reassembled like an infantryman does his rifle. They did not need me but Bob Alde insisted that I be available. Piece by piece it was carried up into a hideaway in a dome at the top of the Tempelhof Airport in West Berlin.

I did not even get to scrutinize my passport. When I got off the plane in Tempelhof, a lady hooked her arm in mine and said, "Let's get off just like we're on a honeymoon." Cameras always snapped pictures of all embarking and departing passengers at Tempelhof. At a hotel they took my passport, I think it was Republic of Ireland (it was a different color than the US ones). I never saw my "wife" again but I was always surrounded by Germans whose job it was to take care of me. I knew this because I spoke fluent German and most of them did not know that before we interacted. Starting at the Army Language School in Monterey, CA, discussed in Chapter 2, when I went back to Arlington Hall Station I continued learning German (and to properly play football, and to dance). My "caretakers," not knowing that I was fluent in German, would let me know subtly that they were not just locals. Some of them, I found out, were actually in the US Army. Immigrants to the US have a shorter time to wait to become a

US citizen if they have spent time in the US services. I think the time was shortened from five years to two years. The hotel clerks, the Herr Obers at the restaurants, the customers at the tanzstuben and bierstuben, and the taxis that picked me up everywhere and took devious routes to Tempelhof and other places, were not just locals. Where the liquid helium and liquid nitrogen came from, I don't know. No one saw it come in and no one saw it go out.

I tell this piece of the NSA operations to emphasize that General Reicheldorfer was dead right: you cannot do a good job and separate COMINT from HUMINT. That was true even in the days when decrypting messages was a large part of NSA activities. But now we are faced with attackers that are not organized as nations, who strap explosives in their bloomers and under their coats, youngsters and oldsters of both genders, blow themselves up and take a few of us with them. Against this new advocacy, HUMINT programs are needed and only the NSA has the wherewithal. I do not know details of actual present day NSA operations but I am sure they are up to this new challenge.

Chapter 5. Conclusions

April 1991: Phil Zimmermann's PGP-1 and its source code were distributed on the Internet as freeware. Within weeks it was being used by rabble groups, all over South America, Africa, and Asia. Some say that the East European countries of Latvia, Estonia, and Lithuania could have never succeeded in a bloodless breakaway form USSR without PGP-1. The military, diplomatic corps, banks, airlines, and large business in general started using PGP-1 in the next year. The RSA Company formed by the inventors of RSA provided similar services at a price. But the main difference in the two was that PGP was the only really strong encryption system that could be trusted because one could take the source code and build it from scratch. The source code in a computer program is the instructions for making the program. PGP was able to use the RSA patented algorithm for the public and private keys because they did not sell the product. It was freeware. Furthermore, they got around the export restrictions (for which the NSA indicted them) by having the source code in a printed form. There was no restrictions on sending printed matter overseas.

June 1992: A world-wide group of first class cryptographers (cryptopunks) got together and made PGP-2 more user friendly, and compatible with Microsoft Windows.

January 1993: Microsoft comes out with Windows-3 and for the first time people who were not computer buffs could and did email and the Internet was off and running in a big way.

May 1993: United States Attorney William Keane informed Zimmermann that he and Kelly Goen (the Johnny Appleseed for spreading PGP) were under investigation for illegal export of munitions.

June 1996: Charges against Phil Zimmermann were dropped.

June 1996: Lt General Kenneth Minihan became the new NSA Director.

August 1996: Microsoft released its completely rebuilt Internet Explorer technology, which included features that were revolutionary for the time. Designed for Windows 95, Internet Explorer 3.0 technology offered useful components that immediately appealed to users, including Internet Mail and News and Windows Address Book.

June 1999: Lt. General Michael Hayden is appointed NSA Director.

What happened between 1996 and 2006 at the National Security Agency is historical proof that what was decided in the setting up of the National Security Agency in 1953 was the seed of a cancer in our government. I repeat from the introduction:

> At 12:01 on the morning of November 4, 1952, a new federal agency was born. Unlike other such bureaucratic births, however, this one arrived in silence. No news

coverage, no congressional debate, no press announce-
ment, not even the whisper of a rumor. Nor could any
mention of the new organization be found in the Government Organization Manual or the Federal Register
or the Congressional Record. Equally invisible were
the new agency's director, its numerous buildings, and
its ten thousand employees. . . . It was the birth cer-
tificate for America's newest and most secret agency,
so secret in fact that only a handful in the government
would be permitted to know of its existence.

This was the seed of a cancer in our government. It also
says in the Introduction that: .The novelty of these ideas was
discussed in the offices of Arlington Hall Station for months
thereafter. It soon became apparent that this was a very reasonable and wise arrangement. It was blatantly realized that
withdrawing Congress's right of oversight was unconstitutional. It was strongly held, though, that the means justified the end because the recent history of World War II had
shown that years and millions of lives were saved by code
breaking and the secrecy thereof. It was imperative that there
not be even a hint that an adversary's messages were being
decrypted. NSA employees were not allowed to tell outsiders
that they worked for the NSA. No contract personnel were
used and all NSA employees were either career civil servants
or career military personnel. We never thought we would see
the day when there would be no need for a code-breaking apparatus in the Government. This is always the danger when
one rationalizes by saying the end justifies the means.

So between 1996 and 1999, this is the way the NSA
adapted:

- In 1999 General Michael Hayden was made NSA
  Director by the President.

- They continued telling the world that this large organization is still used for an extensive code breaking

operation—the big lie. They get away with it because they are free from any scrutiny.

- They triple their size by hiring 70% contract personal. These additional people are used for newly instituted traffic analysis programs, i.e. listen in on and recording all plain text phone conversations and emails.

- They continue to request and harass media people to not use their name or locations under the threat that it would damage national security.

In a question-and-answer session at the National Press Club in Washington, D.C. before an audience consisting largely of journalists, reporter Jonathan Landay of Knight Ridder attempted to preface a question to General Hayden by stating that the Fourth Amendment of the Constitution specifies that you must have probable cause to be able to do a search legally.

Jonathan Landay: "It is my understanding that the Fourth Amendment of the Constitution specifies that you must have probable cause to be able to do a search that does not violate an American's right against unlawful search and seizure."

General Hayden, "The Fourth Amendment actually protects all of us against unlawful search and seizure."

Jonathan Landay, "But the measure is probable cause."

General Hayden, "The Amendment says unreasonable search and seizure!"

Jonathan Landay, "But does it not say 'probable cause'?"

General Hayden interrupts, "No, the Amendment says 'unreasonable search and seizure'!"

Jonathan Landay, "The legal standard is probable cause."

General Hayden, "Let's be very clear, believe me, if there is any Amendment to the Constitution that the National Security Agency is very familiar with, it is the Fourth; and it is the unreasonable search and seizure standard."

The Fourth Amendment says in full:

> The right of the people to be secure in their persons,
> houses, papers, and effects, against unreasonable
> searches and seizures, shall not be violated, and no
> warrants shall issue, but upon probable cause, sup-
> ported by oath or affirmation, and particularly describ-
> ing the place to be searched, and the persons or things
> to be seized.

Surely it's not too much to ask that the officials who are
entrusted with the ability to spy on virtually any electronic
communication have an appreciation of how this amendment
limits that ability. Yet Hayden repeatedly demonstrated that
he does not know the basic language of this key part of the
Bill of Rights. Hayden's response returned to the issue of the
Fourth Amendment:

> "I didn't craft the authorization. I am responding to a
> lawful order, all right? The attorney general has averred
> to the lawfulness of the order. Just to be very clear,
> okay—and, believe me, if there's any amendment to the
> Constitution those employees at the National Security
> Agency is familiar with, it's the Fourth, all right? And
> it is a reasonableness standard in the Fourth Amend-
> ment. So, what you've raised to me—and I'm not a law-
> yer, and don't want to become one—but what you've
> raised to me is, in terms of quoting the Fourth Amend-
> ment, is an issue of the Constitution. The constitu-
> tional standard is 'reasonable.' And we believe—I am
> convinced that we're lawful because what it is we're
> doing is reasonable."

By showing that he was unaware of the "probable cause"
language in the Fourth Amendment, Hayden revealed that his
insistence that it was legal for the NSA to conduct warrant-

less surveillance was not based on even a nodding familiarity with the constitutional issues involved.

To demonstrate that the spread of this cancer is now out of control, The *Washington Post* on July 19, 2010 started an extensive series of stories about the uncontrolled, intense, unknown-to-any-one-person-or-branch-of-government, and runaway security programs. *The Post* called the series "National Security Inc". The two reporters for the exposé are Dana Priest and William M. Arkin. Dana Priest has won numerous awards, including the 2008 Pulitzer Prize for public service for "The Other Walter Reed" and the 2006 Pulitzer for best reporting for her work on CIA secret prisons and counterterrorism operations overseas. William M. Arkin has authored more than a dozen books about the U.S. military and national security. Yet in the whole exposé it was never mentioned that the NSA's pre-1996 function had been rendered obsolete and that is why they could go from all government employees to mostly contractors. The underlying thesis is that after 9/11, the NSA went wild with an expansion using contractors. This thesis is very misleading. The real reason the NSA started their expansion using contract personnel in 1997 was because they had lost their function in cryptography due to world-wide use of PGP and other similar free software used by governments and everybody else.

With nothing else to do in the message interception activity, the NSA switched to an extensive program in traffic analysis and plain text interception. Contract personnel could be used in this less sensitive aspect of message interception. It is easy for an outsider to associate the change in employment policy with 9/11 because money was thrown at them by the Bush Administration to "do something about the terrorists". Of course, this most secretive organization is not going to admit there is little they can do. So they grow a mammoth, secretive contractor-run organization—a perfect example of Parkinson's Law: Work expands so as to fill the time available for its completion.

Ms. Priest was interviewed by Keith Olbermann on the July 20 evening TV show, and did not mention the NSA. Another guest on the show, Frances Townsend, who worked on security as part of the Clinton and G.W. Bush administrations, said that the problem was not so serious because Congress has oversight over all the Agencies (and their half-million new contract employees with top secret clearance).

If you go to the map in the *Washington Post* article, you will see plots of thousands of new facilities all over the United States owned and operated by contract personnel in the business of listening and recording plan text messages. Billions of dollars and 100,000 contract employees with top secret clearances have been added to NSA.

To further show that the intelligence community is unable to ascertain the origin and content of messages, as was stated in the Introduction, consider the postings on www. wikileaks.org/. It is a web operation of about 100 people that work to protect whistle-blower's identity. They routinely publish classified information. They recently published 2000 or so secret documents of the State Department and the U.S. military about our war in Afghanistan. They announced that they will soon publish thousands more. Can NSA find out who these people are? Of course not. Can Congress ask NSA why they don't know about these people? Of course not.

Attempts have been made to free up information on how NSA hoodwinks America by the American Civil Liberties Union. Here is an ACLU statement by James Bamford, the only person who has written extensively about NSA:

January 6, 2006

My decision to join the ACLU lawsuit against the National Security Agency was not only difficult, but painful. During a quarter century of writing about the NSA, including the only two books on the agency and countless articles, I have developed a great deal of respect and even awe for the people who work there. A number of junior cryptologists I came in contact with when I first began writing *The Puzzle Palace* in 1979 had become senior officials by the time I finished the sequel, *Body of Secrets*, in 2001. Some of them had also become friends. During that period, my relationship with the NSA had also changed, from being threatened with prosecution, to being honored with a book signing ceremony at the agency.

In *The Puzzle Palace* I devoted a considerable amount of pages to a long list of illegal and improper activities conducted by the agency during the Watergate period. But in *Body of Secrets* I went to great lengths to explain how the agency had put that past behind it and was now paying strict attention to the law. I even defended the agency on many occasions, including when invited to Brussels to testify before the European Parliament which was looking into whether the NSA was spying on European businesses and passing the intelligence on to American corporations. I expressed my view that they were not. In his book, Chatter, about eavesdropping around the world, Patrick Radden Keefe noted that I have "gone from being the scourge of the NSA to the agency's hagiographer."

But now it appears that the agency has gone full circle, and just as I will defend it when I think it is being wrongly accused, I will just as vigorously come out against it when I believe it has gone over the line.

On June 5, 1970, President Nixon met in the Oval Office with the then director of the NSA, Vice Admiral Noel Gayler, and directed him to begin eavesdropping on Americans. At the NSA, Deputy Director Louis Tordella regarded the change as "nothing less than a heaven-sent opportunity for the NSA." This was in part because the agency had already begun secretly spying on Americans even before Nixon's order. Following the meeting, an "Eyes Only" memorandum entitled "NSA Contribution to Domestic Intelligence" was then drafted and signed by the president authorizing the NSA "to program for coverage the communications of U.S. citizens using international facilities." No warrant or probable cause would be required, the decision on who would be listened to would be made by agency shift supervisors, and anyone's international telephone calls, telegrams, or faxes could be intercepted and distributed. Given the top secret codename "Minaret," among those targeted in the program were large numbers of anti-Vietnam war protesters who were violating no law.

When Operation Minaret was discovered during the mid-1970s, the Justice Department under the Ford administration made the extraordinary decision to launch a secret criminal investigation of the entire agency. Shocked senior officials were given Miranda warnings and investigators came up with 23 possible areas of criminal prosecution. But because of the secrecy of the information involved, and the fact that the law was very vague in this area at the time, they decided against prosecution. Instead, they recommended that the administration and Congress consider enacting laws making such activities illegal and imposing long prison sentences for those who ignore or go around the law.

Because President Nixon attempted to justify his action by citing the then ongoing war in Vietnam, as well as the Soviet nuclear threat of the Cold War, the crafters included a provision that in time of war—including an all-out Congressionally declared war—the NSA is limited to just fifteen days of warrantless eavesdropping. Later, both Republicans and Democrats enacted the Foreign Intelligence Surveillance Act, which required the NSA to obtain a warrant from a special court before eavesdropping on Americans on U.S. soil, and included a penalty of five years in prison for every violation. For three decades, during both Republican and Democratic administrations, the Foreign Intelligence Surveillance Court functioned smoothly and without a single leak, issuing nearly 19,000 warrants and turning down only five. Those few rejections could then be argued de novo before the Foreign Intelligence Court of Review, which has only heard one case in nearly thirty years.

Then in the fall of 2001, NSA director, Lt. Gen. Michael V. Hayden allegedly began ignoring the FISA law. Instead of allowing FISA court judges to decide which Americans should be targeted, as the law required, he secretly gave the responsibility back to agency shift supervisors, as was done during Watergate. And months later, President Bush issued an order approving and continuing the operation, just as President Nixon had done.

What greatly concerns me as is that in the past, when NSA was allowed to operate in absolute secrecy, without oversight, it became a rogue agency. When the agency discovered that another author, David Kahn, was planning to include a chapter about the agency in his book on the history of cryptology, *The Codebreakers*, they secretly placed his name on their watchlist and began monitoring his communications. According to an investigation by the Senate Select Committee on Intelligence, they even considered breaking into his New York house to conduct "clandestine service applications." It may never be known how many other authors and journalists were targeted back then. But with the Justice Department only willing to go after the *New York Times* whistleblower, and not the agency that continues to violate the FISA law, the ACLU lawsuit seems like the only way to find out who's being targeted today.

This law suit was dismissed by the courts. Implicit in what James Bamford is saying is that we have one of the largest agencies of the US Government that does things that some think are illegal. The NSA brought out the same old justification that they used in the past. To wit, unlike any other agency, they cannot allow authorities to know what they do because of their unique need for secrecy in code work. Few people in the courts, Congress, or the populous in general understand that this is not true.

There are many sacred and profound documents, the Old Testament, the Christian Bible, the Koran, the United States Constitution, the teachings of Buddha, and so on. They are sacred for two reasons: because they introduced new ways of looking at life and because these new paradigms have stood the scrutiny and test of time. As a general pattern of history, people started living in close proximally to each other as a result of the invention of agriculture, thus creating civilizations. This was about 5000 years ago. Also as a pattern, civilizations cannot exist without some generally agreed upon rules for interaction of the citizenry. Prior to agriculture, formalized "rules of engagement" were not needed for existence in small hunter-gatherer tribes. As a general pattern, civilizations for the first 3000 years were controlled by belief in the divine right of emperors. Civilizations for the next 2000 years were controlled by religions having to do with the fear of death. In 1492 this all changed. Settlers to the New World were from diverse religious groups. Eventually in the New World a new belief system took form, the Constitution of the United States. The Constitution of the United States is considered more sacred by more people than any other belief system. If you do not think so, just ask people which they would choose to give up, if the need be: the Constitution or their religious institutions.

Constitutional rights were originally only for white men property owners. It has evolved to be for everybody. After the Civil War the amassed wealth of corporations brought them political power. The power resulted in court decisions that declared corporations had all the constitutional rights of people. Similarly, even more wealth and power, amassed after World War II, led President Dwight Eisenhower to warn the nation to beware of the "military–industrial complex."

We have shown in this book that there has been a creeping abolition of Congress's right of oversight of the Executive branch of the government when it comes to operation of the NSA. Few people know this exists. Indeed, few realize, even Congressmen, that no information about any employees of the National. Security Agency, their names or their duties, would be given to Congress under any circumstances. Even the House or Senate Intelligence Committees cannot subpoena employees of the National Security Agency, even if they were given the employees names. As we have explained, originally it was thought necessary that Congress be excluded from the inter-working of the NSA and that Congressional oversight not be allowed. Now the main function of the NSA has vanished—the making and breaking of codes and ciphers for national communications security. Inventions that have changed the world for the last 200 years have been in hardware or the consequences have been in hardware. The secret budget, duties, lack of Congressional oversight, and the natural inclination for the public to not be aware of more sophisticated mathematical invention, has resulted in an NSA with a budget of twice that of Central Intelligence Agency (CIA) and FBI combined; and an extensive diminishing of functions to perform. In addition, they have taken advantage of minimal Congressional oversight to rampantly and illegally compile a database of all American plain text messaging by phone and Internet. Yes, every email and phone conversation you have sent is in their database. But the CIA, FBI, and all other agencies of the US government are subject to Congressional oversight.

Congress needs to enact legislation to make the NSA, like all other agencies, answerable to the people. Power corrupts and absolute power corrupts absolutely.

Appendix A. Some Mathematical Concepts of Cryptography

Modular Arithmetic

Note that 12345 x 64389 x 891463 = 708608075115915. I just picked any three numbers from my computer calculator. Now note that 12345(mod 103) = 88. Go to your desktop calculator and enter 12345, then click the "mod" tab on the top row and then enter 103,.read 88. What this means is that when 12345 is divided by 103 you will get some whole number (actually 119 but you will not know that) with a remainder of 88. Now do the same with the other two numbers, 64389 and 891463. You will get 64389 (mod 103) = 14. You will get 891463 (mod 103) = 101. Now note that the product of these three numbers, 88 x 14 x 101 = 124432; and that 124432(mod 103) = 8. This means that the remainder of 124432 when divided by 103 is 8. I can tell you right off, without calculating that 708608075115915 (mod 103) is 8. Try it on your calculator.

They found out 300 years ago that, if two whole numbers, a times b = c; then a(mod n) times b(mod n) = c(mod n) where n is also a whole number. To use this information, you don't have to know why this is true any more than you need to know why a pencil drops when you let loose of it, in order to put it on the table. It has been doing that for a long time and we can assume it will do it the next time. People have been doing modular arithmetic for 300 years and it works every time. This also holds true for addition and subtraction, but not division. In other words, if a and b are whole numbers and if

ab = c ,

then

a(mod n)b(mod n)=c(mod n) ,

where n is also a whole number. Similarly, if

a + b = c

then

a(mod n)+b(mod n)=c(mod n)

Also

a(mod n)-b(mod n)=c(mod n)

if

a − b = c .

Prime Numbers

A prime number is a whole number that cannot be factored. For example 63 can be factored into 3 x 7 x 3=63. 3 and 7 are prime numbers. 1, 3, 5, 7, 11, 13, 17, 19, 23, 29, 31, 37, 41, . . . 523, 541, . . . 11351, 11353, 11369 and zillions of others are numbers that, when divided by another number will always give a decimal. Google 'prime' on your computer and you will get lists of them.

Greatest Common Divisor

The greatest common divisor of two numbers is the largest number that will evenly divide the two numbers—no decimals. For example the greatest common divisor of 72 and 102 is 6; 6 x 9 = 72 and 6 x 17 = 102. No number larger than 6 will evenly divide 72 and 102. 3 will evenly divide both. 2 will evenly divide both and of course 1 will evenly divide both. There is a systematic way to find the greatest common divisor. It is called the Euclidean Algorithm. Using the above example it goes like this;

$$102 = 72(1) + 30$$
$$72 = 30(2) + 12$$
$$30 = 12(2) + 6$$
$$12 = 6(2) + 0$$

The remainder for each division is divided into the previous remainder until the final remainder is (always) zero. The remainder for the next-to-last step (the last non-zero remainder) is the greatest common divisor (gcd). It is written as (gcd) 102,72 = 6. One more example, I chose two numbers out of the air, 12345 and 678. The Euclidean Algorithm gives,

$$12345 = 678(18) + 141$$
$$678 = 141(4) + 114$$
$$141 = 114(1) + 27$$
$$114 = 27(4) + 6$$
$$27 = 6(4) + 3$$
$$6 = 3(2) + 0$$

The gcd = 3. The largest number that will evenly divide 12345 and 678 is 3.

In cryptography, prime numbers are often used. The gcd of primes is 1. This is another way of defining primes. Also, we will have the situation in crypto when two numbers that are not necessarily primes are called co-primes if their gcd = 1. Most even numbers and primes are co-primes but not always, e.g., gcd 5,10 = 5, not 1   so they are not co-primes.

Extended Euclidean Algorithm

The extended Euclidean algorithm is another form of the Euclidean algorithm described above. In this form, any two whole numbers a and b will always have two associated numbers x and y such that,

$$ax + by = (g.c.d.)a, b \qquad (1)$$

In our case, for use in the RSA encryption system we will be using the situation where E and $(p-1)(q-1)$ in equation (7) below will be co-primes so that

$$(g.c.d.)E, (p-1)(q-1) = 1$$

Fermat's Little Theorem

Fermat's little theorem says that any whole number, raised to the power p-1, (mod p) equals one if p is a prime. In formula form,

$$M^{(p-1)}(\text{mod } p) = 1, \qquad (2)$$

where M is absolutely any whole number (in our RSA crypto algorithm M is the message).

This was discovered by a dead Frenchman, Pierre de Fermat (1601–1665, pronounced *ferma*), in the 1630s. He was supposed to be dead. He was reported dead from the plague. He was not. There were so many dying no one could keep count. It was a good thing, too: we owe him a lot. He was not an outstanding lawyer; he couldn't keep his mind off his hobby. Fermat first presented this formula, dubbed "Fermat's Little Theorem," without proof, in one of his letters in 1640. Proof was much more important before computers because one could not try many examples to test validity. What if someone had asked, "Pierre, how do you know that $17^{102} (\text{mod } 103)=1$?" He would have said, "Are you crazy? Don't you know there is a plague going on? Do you know how many years it would take me to calculate that?" Imagine multiplying 17 by itself 102 times longhand! The answer is 20471918733646472337466285889024453000089615408151825524004841295985107 64874975638890736639985472047292802484386766908712 289. Now we do not have a plague and you can leisurely go to your laptop and bring down the desktop calculator. Enter an arbitrary number, say 17, and then click the x^y key. Then enter 102 and click the = key. Then enter 103 and click the mod key. The answer will be 1.

Euler's Totient Function φ

It would be Leonhard Euler who provided the first published proof a hundred years later. His approach was like this: Take any number, let's say 24 for example, how many numbers smaller than 24 are co-prime with 24 ? They are 1,5,7,11,13,17,19, and 23; 8 of them. All other whole numbers,

2,3,4,6,8,9,10,12,14,16,18,20,21, and 22 have a greater common divisor than 1. Therefore $\varphi(24) = 8$. The way we are going to use this idea in the RSA crypto algorithm is in the form

$$M^{(p-1)(q-1)}(\mod pq)=1, \quad (3)$$

where M is the message and we mind that p and q are primes. Leonhard Euler showed that

$$M^{\varphi(p)\varphi(q)}(\mod pq) = 1$$

in general for any φ. In the RSA encryption algorithm we chose p and q as primes. For any prime the $\varphi(p) = p - 1$ because all numbers less than p are not evenly divisible by p and so there are p-1 of them.

These two men play the pivotal role in our RSA encryption algorithm.

The algorithm goes like this. Suppose somebody has a message M in the form of a number to be encrypted and sent to me. My public keys, E and n, are published on the net at a keyserver.com site for all the world to use in sending me a message. n is the product of two mammoth primes, p and q. No one knows what they are. M is encrypted as,

$$M^{E}(\mod n)=C, \quad (4)$$

and sent to me. This is a one-way street; there is no way to know that C came from M if you don't know what M is. C could have come from lots of numbers other than M. C is the encrypted message. There will exist another number D that will decrypt C back into M as,

$$C^{D}(\mod n)=M.$$

D is my secret key that I and only I know.

If this is true we could raise equation (4) to the D power and also write,

$$\left\{M^{E}(\mod n)\right\}^{D} = \left\{C(\mod n)\right\}^{D}$$

or

$$M^{DE}(\mod n) = C^{D}(\mod n)$$

or

$M^{DE}(\text{mod } n)=M$.   (5)

Finally we can divide both sides by M and have,

$M^{DE-1}(\text{mod } n)=1$.   (6)

Now notice that equation (6) is in the form of Fermat's Little Theorem. Check out equations (5) and (6) using the example from Chapter 4 about buying a chocolate pig with lipstick; we had p=41, q=31, n=1271, E=7 and D=343, and so ED = 2401. Let's say that the message M that we want to encrypt is 3.

M=3. ED=7 x 343

$3^{2401}(\text{mod } 1271)=3$,

and

$3^{2400}(\text{mod } 1271)=1$.

Euler's φ equation, equation (3) and Fermat's equation (6) can be set equal to each other

$M^{(p-1)(q-1)}(\text{mod } pq)=M^{DE-1}(\text{mod } pq)$

because both sides of this equation are equal to 1, We could also raise them to any power because $1^k = 1$

$\left\{M^{(p-1)(q-1)}(\text{mod } pq)\right\}^{k}=\left\{M^{DE-1}(\text{mod } pq)\right\}^{j}$

or

$$M^{k\{(p-1)(q-1)\}}(\text{mod } pq)=M^{j\{DE-1\}}(\text{mod } pq)$$.

There will exist a j and k such that,

$j\{DE-1\} = k\{(p-1)(q-1)\}$.

Put this in the form of the Extended Euclidean Algorithm, equation (1), it becomes,

$j\{DE\} = k\{(p-1)(q-1)\}+j$

remembering that $ax = b\,y + (\text{g.c.d.})\,x,y$.   (1)

In our case E and   (p-1)(q-1) are co-primes so gcd(x,y)=1. So j must be 1. Finally, this gives the equation for finding D in the RSA encryption system of:

$DE = k\{(p-1)(q-1)\}+1$ (7)

remainder	quotients	$x_j = x_{j-2} - q_j x_{j-1}$	$y_j = y_{j-2} - q_j y_{j-1}$
$r_{-1} \equiv \varphi = 12345678$		$x_{-1} = 1$	$y_{-1} = 0$
$r_0 \equiv E = 45629$		$x_0 = 0$	$y_0 = 1$
$r_1 = 25848$	$q_1 = 270$	$x_1 = 1 - 270(0) = 1$	$y_1 = 0 - 270 = -270$
$r_2 = 19781$	$q_2 = 1$	$x_2 = 0 - (1)(1) = -1$	$y_2 = 1 - (-270) = 271$
$r_3 = 6067$	$q_3 = 1$	$x_3 = 1 - (-1) = 2$	$y_3 = -270 - (1)271 = -541$
$r_4 = 1580$	$q_4 = 3$	$x_4 = -1 - (3)(2) = -7$	$y_4 = 271 - 3(-541) = 1894$
$r_5 = 1327$	$q_5 = 3$	$x_5 = 2 - 3(-7) = 23$	$y_5 = -541 - 3(1894) = -6223$
$r_6 = 253$	$q_6 = 1$	$x_6 = -7 - (1)(23) = -30$	$y_6 = 1894 - (1)(-6223) = 8117$
$r_7 = 62$	$q_7 = 5$	$x_7 = 23 - 5(-30) = 173$	$y_7 = -6223 - 5(8117) = -46808$
$r_8 = 5$	$q_8 = 4$	$x_8 = -30 - 4(173) = -722$	$y_8 = 8117 - 4(-46808) = 195349$
$r_9 = 2$	$q_9 = 12$	$x_9 = 173 - 12(-722) = 8837$	$y_9 = -46808 - 12(195439) = -2390996$
$r_{10} = 1 \text{ (g.c.d.)} \equiv \Phi \cdot E$	$q_{10} = 2$	$x_{10} = -722 - 2(8837) = -18396$	$y_{10} = 195349 - 2(2390996) = 4977341$
$r_{11} = 0$	$q_{11} = 2$	$x_{11} = k \approx -18{,}396$	$y_{11} = D \approx 4{,}977{,}341$

D and k are found using the Extended Euclidean Algorithm, knowing E and (p-1)(q-1) . k comes out in the wash but has no practical purpose for encryption. It is D that the owner of this address needs to decrypt messages sent to her.

Let's take the example E=45629 and (p-1)(q-1)=12345678 (just randomly picked numbers). The first thing to do is to make sure these two numbers are co-primes. Note that 12345678/45629 is 270 with a remainder of 25848. Therefore they are co-primes.

The algorithm was developed by D.E. Knuth, author of the famous book, *The Art of Computer Programming*, 1981. The recursion relation here can be found in Vol. 2, Section 4.5.2. It is also explained in many places[19]. The procedure starts with choosing for the recursion relation in the first row $r_{-1} \equiv \varphi$ and $x_{-1} = 1$ and $y_{-1} = 0$ for the third and fourth columns. Similarly in the second row $r_0 \equiv E$ and $x_0 = 0$ and $y_0 = 1$. Then r_{i+2} is the remainder of $r_i = r_{i+1}q_{i+2} + r_{i+2}$

$$12345678(-18396) + 45629(4977341) = 1$$

$$\downarrow \qquad \downarrow \qquad + \qquad \downarrow \qquad \downarrow$$

$$\Phi \qquad k \qquad + \qquad E \qquad D \qquad = 1$$

This is a straightforward computer program to get D from p and q and E. It is the D and E discussed in the RSA algorithm. It is also the D and E alluded to by Diffie and Hellman when they first brought up the idea of public key crypto.[19] But, of course, they had no good way to discover/invent a D and E to do the job. As they said, "We propose some techniques for developing public key cryptosystems, but the problem is still largely open." A year later Rivest, Shamir and Adleman invented and described what is explained in this Appendix.

---

[19] "New Directions in Cryptography," W. Diffie and M. E. Hellman, IEEE *Transactions on Information Theory*, vol. IT-22, Nov. 1976, pp: 644-654.

Appendix B. Public Key Crypto Concepts

Computation Time

0	0	0	0	0
1	0	0	0	1
2	0	0	1	0
3	0	0	1	1
4	0	1	0	0
5	0	1	0	1
6	0	1	1	0
7	0	1	1	1
8	1	0	0	0

Sometimes on the Internet you come across situations where you are ask to write the text that is in a picture such as, **C⌐B⌐** , and you fill in the box with CAB6. It would take a very complicated computer program to do the common sense reasoning that your brain does to decrypt this picture.

All computers do is crunch numbers and in cryptography these days a computer tries different numbers to find the key for encrypting a message. If the message is 1234567 and the encryption program adds this to a 7 digit random number 8741395, with no carrying (mod 10 like they did in the example of World War II Japanese Naval code JN-25); then the coded message is 9975852. This is a random number and there is no way to know the message from it. The details of the computer programs that are used to encrypt messages are known to all; examples DES, IDEA, and BLOWFISH as described below. That is the case because no one would trust a procedure (read program) that someone else did and slipped in their own "trap door." In our example the program adds a random number to the message. An attacker has to try all seven digit numbers up to 9999999 to be sure she has tried them all. But in this case, when she gets to 8741395 and subtracts it from the message 9975852 and gets 1234567, she has a number with a pattern. Of course when the attacker gets to the number 8740000 and subtracts it from the message 9975852, she gets 1235852 and the attacker might recognize a pattern of three consecutive numbers in the message. This is equivalent to the (more complicated) situation of the computer coming out with a word in some language. The number of combinations of 10 things (all digits, 0, 1,2,3,4,5,6,7,8,9) taken 7 at a time, and being allowed to repeat (like 6666666), is 10^7. (Of course you knew that.)

Does that mean that if the computer can check one million subtractions a second, that it would take $10^7/10^6 = 10$ seconds to check them all? No! Because the computer does not "check" numbers, it checks bits. Our Arabic based numbers from 0 through 8 are 0 and 1000 in binary. In other words a binary number with 3 zeros is $2^3 = 8$ in our base 10 numbers. So in binary numbers, what is 10^7? The rule is, to go from base

10 numbers to binary, multiply the superscript by 3.3. (1/log 2). So 10^7 is about 2^{23}. The numbers are 23 binary digits (0s and 1's) long. If the attacker can do a million (bit) operations per second, it will take her $2^{23} / 2^6 = 2^{17}$ seconds or many years. Computers today are a lot faster than that.

Symmetric Ciphers

In explaining symmetric ciphers we intentionally chose a straightforward block cipher JN-25 used by the Japanese Navy during World War II. We chose it to illustrate what a block cipher is, how random numbers are used, how modular arithmetic is used, and how a code book was used for the session keys. The session keys were 5 digits long random numbers. A 5 digit, base 10 number is a 17 digit binary numbers. Today standardized symmetric keys use about 128 bits, equivalent to a forty digit base 10 number.

In public key crypto the session keys are sent along with the message. The session key is encrypted using the RSA algorithm with a 1024 or 2048 or even a mammoth (probably overkill) 4096 bit key. Because the session keys themselves are just random numbers, this is secure. Unless an attacker could find p and q of pq=n in equation (7) Appendix A; i.e., $DE = k(p-1)(q-1)+1$ of the RSA public key, there is no practical way to get the session keys. That is why such a large number is used for the RSA key, 1024 or 2048 bits and only 56 to 128 bits for the session keys.

Common Symmetric Ciphers

A detailed explanation of how the session keys are used in the common symmetric ciphers used in the freeware and commercial versions of PGP is readily available on the Internet. Some of the commonly used and world-wide accepted symmetric ciphers are given here.

DES. The Data Encryption Standard is the oldest common block symmetric cipher. It was selected by the National Bureau of Standards as an official Federal Information Processing Standard for the United States in 1976 and which has subsequently enjoyed widespread use internationally. It is based on a symmetric key algorithm that uses a 56-bit key. The algorithm was initially controversial with classified design elements, a relatively short key length, and suspicions about an NSA backdoor. It is no longer used.

IDEA (International Data Encryption Algorithm) is an algorithm that was developed by Dr. X. Lai and Prof. J. Massey in Switzerland in the early 1990s to replace the DES standard. It uses the same key for encryption and decryption, like DES operating on 8 bytes at a time. Unlike DES though, it uses a 128 bit key. This key length makes it impossible to break by simply trying every key, and no other means of attack is known. It is a fast algorithm, and has also been implemented in hardware chipsets, making it even faster. It was used extensively and successfully in the PGP public key freeware for 15 years or so.

BLOWFISH. Blowfish is a symmetric block cipher just like DES or IDEA. It takes a variable-length key, from 32 to 448 bits, making it ideal for adjustable security uses. Bruce Schneier designed Blowfish in 1993 as a fast, free alternative to the then existing encryption algorithms. Since then Blowfish has been analyzed considerably, and is gaining acceptance as a strong encryption algorithm.

The description of anyone's public key given on www.pgp.server.com gives the details. Mine is

ID OxBA17EEAO	CREATED 2/20/2006
TYPE RSA	EXPIRES Never
SIZE 2048/2048	GROUP No
TRUST Implicit	CIPHER AES 256
VALIDITY Valid	HASH SHA-2 256

| KEYSERVER http://www. pgp.keyserver.com | COMPRESSION ZLIP |

An ID is assigned to all created PGP ciphers. In my case the public key transmission is RSA. The expiration is never. The RSA key is 2048 bits. No group, it is individual. Trust is verified by PGP Corp. The cipher used is AES 256 bit. The plain text is first hashed to eliminate linguistic patterns and put into blocks of equal length; the program for hashing is SHA-2 256 bits.

Bibliography

Bamford, James. *Body of Secrets*, Doubleday, 2001.

Bamford, James. *The Puzzle Palace: A Report on America's Most Secret Agency*, Houghton Mifflin, 1982.

Bamford, James. *The Shadow Factory: The Ultra Secret NSA from 9/11 to the Eavesdropping on America*, Doubleday, 2008.

Blum, William. *Killing Hope: U.S. Military and CIA Interventions since World War II*, Common Courage Press, 1995.

Budiansky, Stephen. *Battle of Wits*, The Free Press, 2000.

Coutinho, S.C. *The Mathematics of Ciphers, Number Theory and RSA Cryptography*, A K Peters, 2001.

Hinsley, Sir Henry & Stripp, Alan. *Code Breakers: The Inside Story of Bletchley Park*, Oxford, 1974.

Holmes, W.J. *Double-Edged Secrets*, Naval Institute Press, 1979.

Kahn, David. *The Codebreakers: The Story of Secret Writing*, Macmillian, 1967.

Lakoff, George & Johnson, Mark. *Philosophy of the Flesh: The Embodied Mind and its Challenge to Western Thought*, Basic Books, 1999.

Layton, Edwin T. *And I Was There*, William Marrow & Co., 1985.

Levy, Steven. *Crypto: How the Code Rebels Beat the Government—Saving Privacy in the Digital Age*, Viking, 2001.

Lewin, Ronald. *Ultra Goes to War*, Hutchinson and Sons, 1978.

Lord, Walter. *Incredible Victory*, HarperCollins Publishing, 1967.

Schneier, Bruce. *Applied Cryptography*, John Wiley and Sons, 1996.

Shorrock, Tim. *Spies for Hire*, Simon and Schuster, 2008.

Vankin, Jonathan & Whalen, John. *The 60 Greatest Conspiracies of All Time*, Citadel Press, 1997.

Wise, David & Ross, Thomas B. *The Invisible Government*, Vintage Books, 1974

http://www.philzimmermann.com/EN/sales/index.html

www.pgp.com

www.ultimate-anonymity.com

http://www.mccone.cc/PGP2.htm#Why

INDEX

A

Acheson, Dean G., 6, 94

Adleman, Leonard, 9, 132, 143, 146, 184

Advanced Research Projects Agency (ARPA), 124-125

Agee, Philip, 105

Air Force Security Service, 8, 85, 88

Aktiebolaget Cryptoteknik, 110

Al Qaeda, 153-155

al-Zawahiri, Ayman, 154-155

Alde, Robert O., 158-161

Allende, Salvador, 7, 103

Amarillo Military Academy, 36

Angleton, James Jesus, 104

Applied Research Projects Agency (ARPA), 124-125

Arlington Hall Station, 8, 24, 27, 39, 71-72, 74-76, 78-79, 81, 83, 85, 88, 93, 96, 157, 161, 165

Armed Forces Security Agency, 95

Army Language School of Monterey California, 72-74, 77, 161

Army Security Agency, 8, 55, 63-65, 67, 69-70, 72, 74, 80, 85, 88, 119

Arosemana, Carlos, 100

Autler, Stanley H., 159

B

Bakhtiar, Shahpour, 115

Balawi, al-, Dr. Humam Khalil Abu-Mulal, 154, 156

Bamford, James, 6, 123, 140, 170, 173, 191

Banzer, Hugo, 102